MACY'S
FOR
SALE

MACY'S FOR SALE

Isadore Barmash

WEIDENFELD & NICOLSON

New York

Published by Weidenfeld & Nicolson, New York
A Division of Wheatland Corporation
841 Broadway
New York, New York 10003-4793

Published in Canada by General Publishing Company, Ltd.

Library of Congress Cataloging-in-Publication Data

    Barmash, Isadore.
       Macy's for sale / by Isadore Barmash. — 1st ed.
         p.   cm.
       Includes index.
       ISBN 1-55584-139-2
        1. Macy's (Firm) 2. Leveraged buyouts—United States.   I. Title.
       HF5465.U6M243 1989   88-29408
       338.8'36138145'0—dc19   CIP

Manufactured in the United States of America

This book is printed on acid-free paper

Designed by Irving Perkins Associates

First Edition

10 9 8 7 6 5 4 3 2 1

CONTENTS

PROLOGUE

In July 1986, the top management and 346 other executives of R. H. Macy, the more-than-century-old department store company, acquired that company through a leveraged buyout costing about $3.7 billion. It was the largest internal buyout of any retailing company in history. Using the company's own cash flow and assets as collateral, the entire executive investment amounted to about $17.5 million, giving the group of 348 executives a 20 percent interest in a company with sales of almost $6 billion, a bargain indeed.

The executive takeover's sparkplug was sixty-year-old Edward S. Finkelstein, chairman of the board and chief executive officer, who had turned Macy's from a cautious, almost nondescript retailer into a "lifestyle" innovator catering to the young and the young-minded. A career Macy man, Finkelstein's efforts in the last decade as its New York and then corporate chief gave the company the best and most consistent profit performance in its history and he was generally recognized as one of the finest merchants of his time.

But in November 1985, he shocked his colleagues and business at large with his proposal to buy the company he had served for thirty-five years. "Macy's should belong to the people who turned Macy's around," he told his associates, who were soon convinced to join him in that effort. It would keep executives from straying, Finkelstein assured everyone; it would motivate them, and best of all it would reward them for their performances. And it would ensure that the retail chain would be able to continue its fine progress by having the consistent and stable management it needed.

But there were those who suspected that the real spur was personal profit. Ordinarily, leveraged buyouts are led by managements joined by outside investors when a company is in financial difficulty, needs new capital, or is threatened by an outside takeover. None of these factors existed at Macy's.

What shocked many people—the owning Straus family perhaps most—was that Ed Finkelstein, his closest associate, Mark Handler, and the top tier of the 346 had all been such devoted company men and women. At no point prior to 1985 had there been any indication that that group meant to break the barrier between old money and those who wanted new money, to breach the subtle class distinction of the proprietary group and the salaried group, to take what was only minimally theirs and turn it into a substantial holding of their own, or to give thousands of longtime shareholders a one-time opportunity to sell their shares and turn the company into a private enclave.

In Finkelstein's case, the role reversal was a special surprise. He had been well rewarded, earning more than $780,000 a year, with lavish deferred compensation, perquisites, a New York apartment, and other amenities. It was as if the brightest boy in the class, the one who earned all the A's and received all the awards on Class Day, suddenly announced he was buying the school.

But Finkelstein, Handler, and their group were a product of their time—a time of mergers, of Wall Street's endless gyrations and fall, of confrontation and endlessly litigious activity. It was a time of pressures and individual floundering that inevitably pounded out one theme to everyone: "If I don't take care of myself, who will?"

Yet even the buyout of their own company wasn't enough. On February 29, 1988, when Federated Department Stores was fighting a hostile takeover bid from Campeau Corporation, a Canadian builder, Ed Finkelstein stepped in as a "white knight" contender to face-off against Campeau. Macy's still was more than $2 billion in debt from its own leveraged buyout, but the group was willing to take on another $6 billion debt to buy the owners of Bloomingdale's, Abraham & Straus, Filene's, Bullock's, Burdine's, and other well-known stores. A new battle ensued, leading to a confrontation in which Finkelstein, finally involved in an outside takeover, found himself bested, though he gained two new divisions.

This book tells the story of Macy's managers and their leveraged buyout, the newest and most controversial device in the modern financial armament. It is an unauthorized book, written without the cooperation of the buying group, but my own twelve-year exposure to them, and to many who know them, has been of great help in this project, buttressed by new reporting and research over a fifteen-month period.

I want to thank everyone who helped, who gave me their time and who contributed their experiences and thought. Particularly I want to express my gratitude to those at Weidenfeld & Nicolson: Dan Green, publisher; John Herman, editor-in-chief; and William Strachan, senior editor who worked most closely with me; and to Michael Cohn, the literary agent who put us all together. Nor can I forget all my colleagues at *The New York Times*, a wonderful group of professionals and friends.

But, above all, I want to express my gratitude and love to Sarah, my wife, for her support and understanding in all those tense, turbulent months.

I. B.

MACY'S
FOR
SALE

CHAPTER ONE

TWO ENCOUNTERS, HEATED BY RHETORIC

On a November morning in 1985, Edward S. Finkelstein, the chairman of the board and chief executive officer of R. H. Macy & Company, stared out at four hundred or so shareholders. Many were current Macy executives or other employees, retirees and others who had invested in Macy's for years. He knew, as his whole team did, that there was something of a family feeling among them in regard to Macy's—Mother Macy's. He knew it was the same at AT&T, General Motors, Sears Roebuck, any giant company with many thousands of shareholders. It was hard to tell how strong it was with those facing him, but it would make his job even more difficult. And as he took them in, they gazed back with bright, expectant eyes, almost as if they had forgotten—or was it overlooked or accepted?—what he had done.

"On behalf of the directors and the management of the corporation, I would like to welcome you to this one hundred and twenty-seventh year of operations," he began. "We are happy to see so many of you here. We are grateful to the many shareholders who turned in their proxies. . . .

"Before we proceed with the business of the morning," Finkelstein said, "I know that you will agree with me that these proceedings should record the fact that Jack I. Straus, the honorary chairman and director emeritus, a sixty-four-year Macyite, died in September of this year. Mr. Straus was president and chief executive of the corporation from 1940 to 1956, chairman of the board and chief executive officer from 1956 to 1968. During the period of 1968 to 1976, he was chairman of the executive committee of the board. He served as honorary chairman and a director emeritus from 1976 until his death. Mr. Straus was present at the cornerstone laying of the Broadway building of the Herald Square store at the age of two in 1902. He joined Macy's in 1921 directly after graduation from Harvard College. In his sixty-four-year association with Macy's, Jack Straus was a compelling advocate for integrity, value, and quality in relationships with our customers and suppliers. He constantly challenged his associates to be the best. In June of this year, he attended his sixty-fourth consecutive, Twenty-Five-Year Club dinner and he shared with the group his view of our business. He attended every Thanksgiving Day parade since the first in 1927. Jack Straus will be missed by his employees and his associates. The standards he set for speaking out for the best interests of our customers are ingrained values that we will carry on as a lasting memorial to his life. . . ."

As the meeting's chairman eulogized Straus, some in the audience turned their gaze on the director who sat on the dais at the extreme right of the speaker. Kenneth Straus, the son of Jack Straus, a longtime director and former senior vice-president, stared solemnly out at the audience as Finkelstein recalled his father's tenure. Only a few knew what had occurred among the directors several months earlier, and they could not help but marvel at Finkelstein's composure.

At a board meeting five months before, Finkelstein had presented his proposal for a management group that he headed to purchase Macy in a leveraged buyout. The announcement had surprised most of the directors, but it was Jack Straus who had risen to his feet in rage. Tall, courtly, and low-key, the senior member of the Straus family, which had long owned Macy before it went public, was livid. His red face contrasted sharply with his shaky hands and evident frailness. "Macy's will never be sold while I'm alive!" he shouted.

After a short pause, Finkelstein resumed, "Now I want to get on with the business of the meeting. I want to introduce Mark Handler—get up, Mark—Mark is president and chief operating officer of the corporation."

To those who knew him well, "Get up, Mark" seemed to epitomize the chairman's attitude toward his president. The handsome, dapper Handler, fifty-two years old and much loved within the Macy organization for his ability to understand and empathize, rose. If his smile seemed a bit empty to the critical, perhaps it was because Handler had learned and even enjoyed his role as Finkelstein's alter ego. For years, as their careers had marched in tandem—Handler always a step or two behind—Finkelstein had appeared to become somewhat more peremptory toward his number two. But there was no doubt that each had helped the other succeed, molding themselves to each other, though Handler did so more.

Finkelstein now reeled off a list of the other directors whom the shareholders would either reelect or reject. At sixty, he exuded a well-earned self-confidence, secure in his role at the very pinnacle of the department store business. Chunky—partly because he was an inveterate sweets-nosher—he was of medium height, thick in the middle, with warm, brown eyes and brown hair. He spoke in a vibrant, semibaritone, well hiding his nervousness. No one knew what could arise at an annual shareholders' meeting of a prominent company, especially with some of the demonstrative types who loved to dominate such an event with needling questions. As he called each name, Finkelstein paid somewhat more attention to the inside directors, those Macy executives on the board who were part of the buying team, curious whether any of them would show any signs of pressure.

"Arthur Reiner." Chairman and chief executive of the Macy's New York division, the flagship of the four divisions, forty-five years old, Reiner was a compact, highly controlled man, with eyes narrowed in a careful, wary face. He was a loyal Finkelstein team member to the core. To critics, he seemed the extreme of the corporate species, an unemotional, remote type, untouched by the human problems of others. But to others, his coolness was just a defense, for he had the toughest job of any of the four division heads, the executive who had been handed the very division that Finkelstein himself had turned around.

"Robert N. Friedman." Chairman and chief executive of the Bamberger's New Jersey division, at forty-four, "Bobby" Friedman was a lean, intense, hyperactive man, increasingly considered the best soft-goods merchant in the organization and a particular favorite of the corporate chairman. Friedman and Reiner headed two of the three big, $1 billion sales divisions, but they had totally different personalities. Where his New York counterpart moved with slow deliberation, Bobby walked quickly, poked into everything, spoke incessantly. There was little doubt to this observer that one of the two would someday be Finkelstein's successor as corporate chief.

"Herbert Friedman." Chairman and chief executive of Macy's

Atlanta division, formerly known as Davison's, Friedman, at sixty-two years old, was the senior division head, who had already indicated that he wanted to retire in 1987. After a long struggle to keep pace with and preferably overtake the bigger Rich's department store chain in Atlanta, Friedman had willingly accepted Finkelstein's game plan of upscale targeting and show business presentation that had already succeeded in the three other divisions and had given it his utmost push. The results had been good, and Finkelstein was grateful to, if unexcited by, the genial, polished merchant who seemed like an older brother, even perhaps an uncle or father, to the other divisional heads.

Though his name wasn't called, Harold D. Kahn, chairman and chief executive of Macy's California division, based in San Francisco, sat in the audience, his eyes fixed with intensity on his colleagues on the board. He had been assured that he would join them soon. He would be filling a seat that had been vacated in 1985 by Philip Schlein, who lost a battle with Finkelstein over merchandising policy in the California division and abruptly resigned. Kahn, at forty the youngest of the divisional chiefs, had come to California after serving as the Atlanta division president. He had been carefully schooled by Finkelstein, and was aflame with the chairman's merchandising religion. Lanky, restless, tough, and demanding, with a lingering Brooklyn accent, the boyish Kahn was the latest Finkelstein discovery, a star plucked from the ranks.

Asking the shareholders to withhold their applause until all directors were named, the chairman also called out those who were former Macy executives and other outside directors. The former Macyites included Donald B. Smiley, the seventy-year-old former chairman and chief executive of R. H. Macy, Finkelstein's predecessor and now a director of some of the nation's most prominent corporations. In that role, the tall, quiet, almost phlegmatic Smiley was both a kingmaker and a king remover, but he was said to have a steel-trap mind under his somewhat somber exterior, and he was also very high on Finkelstein. Kenneth H. Straus, sixty years old, the retired chairman of Macy's corporate buying division and former corporate senior vice-president was also cited. Although his late father had bitterly opposed the management buyout offer, Kenneth Straus had kept a calm exterior. He had by far the largest share of Macy stock on the board, 719,000 shares against Finkelstein's 143,000 and Don Smiley's 105,000. It was suspected that he had mixed emotions—he respected Finkelstein and Handler but still harbored a family loyalty that certainly included a proprietary feeling about the company. Another director, who was still employed at Macy, was James O. York, the fifty-eight-year-old president of R. H. Macy Properties and corporate senior vice-president, planning and development. A widely respected real estate executive in the retailing business, he, too, was a devoted Finkelstein team member.

A little more meeting housekeeping followed before Finkelstein plunged into what would be the principal issue of the day and what everyone was waiting to hear. He pitched in briskly, not faltering once in a five-minute oration.

"I guess most of you know that on October 21, Mark Handler and I and other members of Macy's senior management announced that we intend to make a leveraged buyout proposal in which subject to arranging requisite financing, Macy shareholders would receive $70 in cash for each share of Macy's approximate 51.2 million outstanding common shares.

"We contemplate that a large number of other members of the company's management will also be offered the opportunity to participate.

"At that time," he continued, "we said that we would formally present the proposed transaction for consideration by Macy's board of directors when necessary financing has been arranged. Since that date, senior management together with our financial adviser, Goldman Sachs & Company, have proceeded toward arranging the required financing. We have been admonished by legal counsel not to comment further on the proposed transaction at this time. So neither I nor any director can address the subject further nor can we entertain any questions about it.

"You may be sure that we intend to make a further public announcement when the proposed transaction has been formally presented for consideration to Macy's board. The board, as you know, has appointed a specific committee to consider the proposal when it is made and has retained its own financial and legal advisers," Finkelstein said.

Since shareholder approval was required to consummate such a transaction legally, he went on, "A shareholder's meeting will be held at an appropriate time. There will then be full consideration of the matter and shareholders will have the opportunity to vote on the transaction at that time. We have again made arrangements with the hotel to serve a sandwich luncheon after the meeting is over. You are all invited to stay."

If those in the audience brightened at the bit of positive news, he pushed ahead with a little more for those skeptics who listened to him. "Those of you who regularly attend these meetings know that we do not discourage questions or discussions relevant to our business," he said, "so long as they are pertinent to a particular addenda item then before the meeting."

But at that point Finkelstein steeled himself. He knew that comment would be ignored by the professional shareholders' advocates who always showed up at meetings of companies of major exposure. He was surprised to see that both Gilberts were there, the more diplomatic Lewis, who sometimes could be surgically abrasive, and John, the younger brother, who appeared indiscriminately so when he lost his temper. And there was Evelyn Y. Davis, the Washington gadfly who infuriated women by her scorn and who was in turn infuriated by them when they reacted to her withering remarks. "You're jealous of my looks!" she would snap, "because you're so ugly!" But her bark was often worse than her bite, as was the Gilberts'. Finkelstein, having already chaired a number of Macy annual meetings, knew that they had the right to speak for themselves and other shareholders; that was known as "corporate democracy." But he sensed that some disturbing moments lay ahead—and he wasn't wrong.

The Gilberts, whether consciously or by accident, promptly played the "good guy, bad guy" routine. Rising first, Lewis wanted to know if any bylaw changes had been made since the last annual meeting. Marvin Fenster, the corporate secretary and general counsel, replied that several of a "routine and minor" nature had been made, and under Gilbert's prodding, he detailed them. When John Gilbert took the floor microphone, he introduced himself, adding, "The other half of the team. It's rare for the two of us to show up at a meeting, but I thought it was important for me to attend since this might be Macy's last meeting."

John inquired how many shareholders Macy's had among its employees. He brushed aside Fenster's superficial rejoinder that the proxy listed the officer shareholders by insisting that he wanted to know how many other Macyites were shareholders. When Fenster tentatively responded, "That may be private information," John snapped, "You haven't gone private yet!" The two became locked in a short shouting match. John demanded, "Well, how many shareholders get lost, do you know that?" Finkelstein stepped in with the disclosure, "There are about 11,000 shareholders and about 130 of them are lost. That's about 1 percent and I'm told it's a low figure." Many large public corporations lose contact with some shareholders through death or transfer and Macy's loss was actually about average.

Between the brothers Gilbert, Evelyn Davis had her few moments and she took dead aim at Finkelstein. "The buyout is just a sellout! I have it on good authority that Donald Trump and/or Alfred Taubman are behind it for the real estate!" If Finkelstein was stunned at the charge that two of the nation's best-known real estate developers had engineered his leveraged buyout, he didn't show it. He had become almost inured to Evelyn Davis from prior meetings although she had always insisted, "I really like you, Ed."

But the tone had been set. Although the vast majority of share-holders sitting there were mute—after all, how could employee shareholders risk their jobs by rising to question management's buyout?—the meeting's chairman and the directors knew that the three shareholder advocates would not pull any punches, and they worried that these few protesters might encourage others to summon up their courage.

"Ed, I've liked you more than any other Macy chief executive," Evelyn Davis loudly told Finkelstein, "but I am very disappointed that you are trying to buy this company. Seventy dollars a share is too small—it should be $100!" Loud applause from the audience greeted this. "I love you, but I hope you don't get the money to do this deal!" she added.

"Don't love me so much!" responded Finkelstein, grinning.

The next speaker from the floor was more moderate but equally annoyed. He said his name was Charles Tanenbaum and he was speaking for his wife, Mary, who had 2,500 shares of Macy stock and had been a shareholder since 1944. "I am disturbed at the length of time since the buyout was proposed more than a month ago," he said, "during which an increasing amount of the company's stock has been passing to Wall Street, mainly to arbitragers, because of doubt and uncertainty about the buyout. I also want to address myself to two of the directors up for reelection, Mr. Reiner and Bob Friedman, who are among the buyout group. And I raise a serious point about whether they can be reelected as directors. They are heads of their respective store divisions and there is no harm in their functioning in that capacity, but that they should sit on the board of directors to consider a proposal and that they should be reelected after that proposal is public is a troublesome question. Might I have counsel's opinion on that subject?"

Marvin Fenster, the general counsel and himself a member of the buyout group, responded. "I really have no problem with them standing for reelection. As you know, the outside directors are a special committee to pass on this matter. They have retained financial and legal advisers. To the extent at all that this could be considered a potential conflict, that is the device that we have hit upon to take care of the question."

Tanenbaum resumed. "I defer to your point that discussion of the buyout may be inappropriate at this time," he said, "but I am troubled by two things. It seems likely that the company will attempt to sell off some of its assets, stores or shopping centers, in order to pay for its assets. But information of that nature is being withheld. At the same time, the stock has fluctuated widely since the buyout was announced last month and yet in effect is a pressure on stockholders. Yet we stockholders are being asked to make a decision based on knowledge that you have and we don't have. To refuse information to us and to hide behind a lawyer's blackout troubles me."

Shareholders applauded with enthusiasm, but Fenster was equal to the occasion. "Mr. Tanenbaum, when the transaction has jelled," he said, "there will be a voluminous proxy statement in which all the questions you asked will be totally exposed. That's why the Securities and Exchange Commission exists and in fact they do a very vigorous job of enforcing. All the information that you are asking for will be in there. It is quite premature to have all that discussed at a forum of this nature."

"Of course, you cannot provide us with the full details," Tanenbaum conceded. "But obviously information is circulating on the street that causes the fluctuation in the stock. Those arbitragers who are buying millions of shares must know more than is being shared with us. And it's a question why we aren't entitled to know as much as the arbitragers because precisely what you are doing, if you are shifting loyal stockholdings—as I said, my wife has been a Macy stockholder for forty years and it is our largest single holding—while we sit and watch the market fluctuating and wonder is this the time to get out or is it? I don't think you are sharing with the stockholders—"

"Mr. Tanenbaum," Finkelstein interrupted. "We are sharing no information with arbitragers, as you can imagine. Thank you very much. I think we should proceed—"

"You may not be yourselves but certainly information is circulating," Tanenbaum came back. "Some of you in the buyout must know more than you are telling us. And for you to say that you won't share personal knowledge that you have in the buyout, it seems to me that it is inappropriate for you to stand up and chair a meeting and put that kind of blackout on it and you know it yourself!" He was greeted by the biggest round of applause of the meeting up to that point. Few in the audience apparently knew what arbitragers were. If they did, they would have appreciated Tanenbaum's concern. Arbitragers thrive on inside information, buying a stock when it is low in price and then, buttressed by well-founded information, quickly selling it when it rises.

The needling continued. "I notice according to the proxy statement that you have two sons in the business," observed Lewis Gilbert. "Do you have other sons or daughters to put into the business?"

This brought some laughter but Ed Finkelstein saw no humor in it. "Is that meant to be one of the other guns smoking that you brought your brother along to shoot with?" he demanded. His voice was tight with anger, although his syntax was faulty. "I'm not answering that question because I don't believe it deserves an answer. I don't like the tone of it."

"Well, I think it certainly deserves an answer."

"I see no need or reason to answer it."

"I want the record to show," Gilbert said, "that you have refused to answer that question."

"Okay, and I want it to show that you asked it in the way you have," Finkelstein retorted.

Intermittently, Evelyn Davis kept asking if it was true that the management buyout was really being engineered by Donald J. Trump, the dynamic New York real estate developer, and by A. Alfred Taubman, the shopping center builder who had recently bought Woodward & Lothrop, the Washington, D.C., department store chain. Finkelstein had disdained answering the question. When she once again demanded an answer to that "before you go private," the chairman refused. John Gilbert, who occasionally fought with Mrs. Davis at meetings, now pitched in to support her. "Remember, Mr. Finkelstein, you're still an employee of the stockholders. Jack Straus, in my opinion, was a marvelous chairman. He was terrific. I think he would turn over in his grave if he knew what you were doing to the stockholders."

"You have no right to say that!" Finkelstein shouted.

When John Gilbert promptly followed with a question on why all the Macy directors did not sign a recent statement to the SEC, Marvin Fenster said that a number of them had granted power-of-attorney rights to Finkelstein. But the chairman was already upset over the business about his sons and saw in John Gilbert's point another effort to malign him. He told Gilbert that he had his answer from Fenster and that he, Finkelstein, didn't like the inference of misconduct. The two suddenly began shouting at each other until Gilbert asked, "Do we have a code of ethics for employees?"

"Yes, we do."

"Then the code of ethics should be the same for the officers and directors," Gilbert said.

"It is."

"Then they should all sign the 10-K statement [for the SEC] and follow the law. And I'll stop there for the time being."

"I think it's time," Finkelstein said.

There was a smattering of applause, perhaps equally for both men. But Finkelstein's worst fears seemed to have been realized. He appeared rattled. When a vote was being taken on the election of directors, he asked nervously, "Has everyone completed his or his ballot?" He added, in a low voice, "Her ballot."

While the tallies were being made on the four proposals, he delivered his annual report to the stockholders and it was evident that he was pulling himself together. He read smoothly and confidently and one could only respect his self-discipline.

Macy's 1985 fiscal year, ended August 3, was the second best in the company's history, he said, although its net earnings were 15 percent lower than the 1984 peak of $222 million. In the first quarter of the new fiscal year, he reminded the shareholders, net earnings of $42.7 million were 36 percent higher than the October quarter of the year before. "This brought the company's earnings back to a level just short of the record $43 million achieved two years ago," he said. And first-quarter sales of $1.1 billion topped the previous year's by 8.7 percent, Finkelstein added.

He said that the company was more than on track with its five new stores in southeast Florida and five in the Houston and Dallas metropolitan area. Referring to two new units in Houston and Dallas and two in northern California, Finkelstein said, "We are very pleased with the initial customer response to these stores and it provides us with continued confidence that our strategy for store placement, design, and merchandising is correct. Our concept of a new store involves making an immediate, dramatic, and meaningful statement to the customers."

But he went on: "Of course, we are doing a great deal more than just opening large and attractive stores. Our stores have to be staffed with knowledgeable and service-oriented people. Our stores have to be stocked with current fashionable goods that give our customers quality and value day in and day out. We will continue to explore these fundamentals of our business—questioning, probing, experimenting, challenging our result and, hopefully, improving the operations of Macy's business."

He then touched on the point that he had insistently used as the reason for the buyout. "But the one dimension which distinguishes the Macy organization from its competitors," he said, "are the numbers of highly talented retail professionals we have been able to attract and who we must retain. This is our primary strength; we have worked hard and will continue to work hard on this aspect of our business."

Finkelstein, who had been stung by criticism over the 1985 earnings drop, closed on an optimistic note. "We are confident that the earnings decline in 1985, after nine straight years of improvement," he declared, "was an aberration, and that Macy's has resumed its growth trend."

He perked up afterward, inspired as always by his own sterling record. Even Lewis Gilbert seemed to turn friendly and diplomatic. And when John Bollis, a holder of preferred stock, wondered how Ed Finkelstein would be able to sleep at night knowing that the ghost of Evelyn Davis hovered near him, Mrs. Davis called out, "I think his wife might mind." And Finkelstein put in, "As long as she's a ghost." It brought the biggest round of laughter of the meeting.

And then Bollis, who was initially angry about the low value of his preferred shares in contrast with the common, became more light-hearted, pointing to one director. It was Beverly Sills Greenough, the general director of the New York City Opera and a former international opera diva who quietly sat on the dais. "I suggest that at this last Macy annual meeting," Bollis said, "Beverly Sills sing 'Auld Lang Syne' and we all join in."

The mingled applause and laughter was thunderous. Although Mrs. Greenough did not accommodate the request, she gave Finkelstein a pert look. The song might not have been sung, but anticipated nostalgia already hovered in the room.

If it was a tense, nervous time for Ed Finkelstein—so much depended on whether the lavish words of praise heaped on him from the institutional lenders and large investors would really be more than just words—it was also an uneasy time for the nation's retail business. The sluggish 1984 Christmas shopping season had spilled over into 1985. Women shoppers only wanted bargains and male shoppers were even less prone to spend time in stores than they usually did. Except for occasional busy hours, shopping malls everywhere appeared to be only a place where young people congregated, sipping Cokes and beer while playing boom boxes and darting around irritated security guards. Seeking to generate store traffic, worried merchants kept cutting prices, knowing it would reduce their profit margins but unable to come up with any more strategic methods. Suppliers displayed a tougher, more independent attitude, no longer willing to carry big inventories to satisfy merchants' whims and less dependable, smaller orders. While imports of all manner of soft and hard lines were flooding the country, Washington was reluctant to annoy its trading partners by imposing restrictions. Retail company earnings reflected the sluggish sales. Everyone wondered when the economic recovery that the Reagan administration predicted would materialize.

The crunch heated up competition. New forms of retailing rivalry sprouted. After a decade of decline, boutiques were back in and specialized stores of all kinds appeared to be the best approach to skittish, demanding customers. Mergers were in the air, accompanied by the rise of some dramatic new players on the retail scene. Finkelstein could not help noting with mingled interest and apprehension the push of such merchant wheeler-dealers as Leslie H. Wexner, who had within two decades parlayed one tiny women's store into a twelve-hundred store chain, and who only a year earlier had made an abortive, but noisy attack on Carter Hawley Hale Stores, the Los Angeles holding company owning Neiman-Marcus, Bergdorf Goodman, and the Broadway stores, southern California's biggest chain of department stores. Or Milton Petrie, the eighty-year-old dynamo and owner of about one thousand women's shops who publicly declared, "Before I cash in, I'm gonna buy one of the big department store chains." Or David C. Farrell, the tough, acquisitive chief of May Department Stores of St. Louis, who was spoiling to make a merger. Or Thomas M. Macioce, chairman of Allied Stores Corporation, who wanted to generate a major acquisition as a fitting epitaph to his impending retirement. He could be especially dangerous because he enjoyed a close relationship with Edward J. DeBartolo, the country's most successful shopping center developer. And there was Howard Goldfeder, the chairman of Federated Department Stores, of Cincinnati, which operated Bloomingdale's and Abraham & Straus, Macy's two biggest rivals in the New

York and New Jersey markets. The crusty Goldfeder needed to perform a dramatic act to shore up his own troubled business empire. Buying another major company, especially at a time when the stock market was pushing toward a 1,500 peak in the Dow Jones industrial average, seemed to represent a panacea to corporate chiefs.

And there were other wolves howling in the woods. The Haft family, who had built a highly remunerative Dart Drug chain, sold it at a large profit, and launched the Crown books chains with sharp discounts (irking other booksellers), was known to be eyeing retail and other companies; Irwin Jacobs, the Minneapolis tycoon, who had a golden touch with green-mailing other companies; Carl Icahn, who had done similarly with Marshall Field & Company and other retailers; Laurence and Robert Tisch, always sensitive and usually successful in making investments that sometimes would emerge as takeovers. And others of that vein, such as Ivan Boesky and Paul A. Bilzerian, not to mention the Wall Street investment bankers with young and not-so-young partners and managing directors so eager to garner seven-figure incomes by seeking out likely merger targets. God alone knew how many of those fevered types hovered over their office computers, running corporate operating figures up and down the screen to spot chinks or hidden assets just waiting to be scooped up. It was enough to keep a chief executive sipping coffee in a darkened kitchen at three in the morning.

Early in 1985, Finkelstein had been much stirred by an article he read in the *Wall Street Journal*. The piece asserted that any corporate chief executive who didn't make it his business to learn finance was simply asking for trouble. The advice cut deeply into Finkelstein's consciousness. Since he had become Macy's corporate chief in August 1980, he had tried to learn and expose himself to as many of the aspects of the company as he could. He was sensitive, too, about his knowledge. In October 1980, for example, when I interviewed him and Mark Handler, Finkelstein bristled at the questions "Don't you think it is odd, maybe even a little risky, that both you and Handler as heads of Macy are both merchants? Shouldn't one of you be an operating man to balance the skills needed to run a company?"

These were innocuous questions, at best, aimed at deriving some elaboration on how the new team would operate. But Finkelstein, who was generally considered one of the finest merchants in retailing, responded with a touch of ire, "I'm not a merchant. I'm a rounded executive. So is Mark. You shouldn't think of us as just merchants. That's wrong."

The *Journal* article, however, set a fire under him. Always a fast learner, he quickly absorbed as much he could from reading on finance. He contacted the people at Goldman Sachs & Company, Macy's investment bankers, and other banking people. And what he learned convinced him that his fears that Macy might become a target of a takeover attack were valid. There were options that one could take, primarily to enhance a company's assets so that it would represent a strong, rather than weak, target, and, of course, he could leave Macy's. But that would not remove Macy from attack and might, in fact, render it even more open to takeover.

Macy could sustain its independence by selling off some of its properties to make it less attractive, restructuring in other ways that would provide the same benefits, buying up a big portion of its stock, making a bid for itself or seeking an amenable partner. He pondered these and other more esoteric possibilities, discussing them with Goldman Sachs and other friends on Wall Street. At no point, he told me later, did he discuss it with Mark Handler or any on the Macy team. He wanted to be sure, first.

And finally he was. He would do the toughest thing, but the one most likely to preserve Macy, keep his people from straying, fend off any acquisitors and . . . make them all rich. "The ones who have done the job at Macy's," he told himself then and repeated it many times afterward to others, "are the ones who ought to own Macy's."

There was another dimension to that. He was, as he explained later to friends, "getting on to sixty years old." After a thirty-five-year career with the company, he held less than 1 percent of the stock despite generous stock options. And most of his closest colleagues at Macy's owned even less and were being constantly badgered to go elsewhere with very sweet inducements, as he was. It all added up to an internal buyout. And, if necessary, he would take the lumps that came with it.

But the seven months between the penultimate meeting in 1985 and the final one in 1986 were so brutal, frustrating, and full of disappointment and discovery of hypocrisy that he came close more than once to packing in the whole business. But he didn't. He stuck to his convictions; he sold the proposition to all manner of big lenders, even the Japanese and Europeans; he discovered new friends, new adherents. And, finally, when he stood again at the podium at the Penta Hotel in Manhattan in June 1986, he was himself again, more poised and more confident than ever.

* * *

The players were the same as at the previous meeting and they held forth pretty much as before. But Finkelstein and others sensed that while they were just as biting, some of the heart had gone out of their fight. The inside word, which obviously had filtered through the room in the minutes before he had started the meeting, was that the Macy crowd already had it sewn up. They had the votes, more than the three-quarters of the outstanding common shares needed to approve the buyout. If true, and Finkelstein knew that it was, the war was over. The only thing left was how acrid the final battle of words would be.

Most of the shareholders who spoke registered similar complaints. They had patiently stuck with Macy's management through thick and thin, accepting the rise and fall of the stock. Now that Macy's fortunes had begun to brighten, they would no longer be able to retain their investment or make money on it when they could. That wasn't right, was it? In addition, by being forced to sell their Macy stock in the proposed buyout, they would have to pay back in income taxes much of the profits they had made on the stock. That, they said, wasn't right, either.

Those complaints had been formalized shortly after the previous meeting by Suzanne Geisler, a New York shareholder, in a class action suit in the New York State Supreme Court in Manhattan. She had charged that the then $70-a-share offer "would freeze out shareholders from the opportunity to share in the turnaround and growth anticipated by management. The company is poised for a dramatic turnaround." She called the $70-a-share offer "fraudulently low" and asked that the leveraged buyout proposal be set aside. The price of the offer, she contended, wasn't all that it seemed. Macy had invested some $35 million in store renovations in the fiscal year ended August 3, 1985, which had cut earnings for the year by about 14.7 percent. This, she contended, in turn caused Macy's common stock to fall from a year's high of $63.25 to a low of $38.50. But, seeing this, she charged in her suit, Macy's management proposed a $70-a-share buyout offer, knowing it was only slightly higher than the recent market price. "It is an attempt to advance management's personal interests and finances at the expense of public shareholders," Mrs. Geisler charged.

Her suit also contended that many of Macy's properties were being carried on its books at only a fraction of their fair market value. Among such properties, she cited the New York flagship store at Herald Square, stores in San Francisco and Atlanta, as well as property in many "well-positioned" shopping malls.

Although her suit failed, her claims were echoed in some of the shareholder comments to Finkelstein. But it took Charles J. Tanenbaum, the retired attorney who had held forth at the prior meeting, to belabor Finkelstein on her and his own behalf. Repeatedly, he challenged the chairman on one point after another. Holding aloft the 150-page proxy statement Macy had prepared for the meeting, he said that he couldn't understand why Macy's outside directors had changed their minds several times. At first, he said, they had rejected a $68-a-share offer, then accepted a $70 bid, and when that was reduced $2 a share, they had accepted that. Registering further confusion with a wild shake of his head, Tanenbaum said that when the leveraged buyout proposal was first announced, the outside directors failed to disclose that they had originally spurned the management proposal. "Why didn't they say something at the time?" he wondered. But an attorney representing Macy's outside directors, asked by Finkelstein to respond, said that the outside committee did not reject the proposal and that Tanenbaum had "misread the proxy statement." All that was necessary was a press release that was issued at the time, he said.

But the proxy, as someone familiar with it might have found during the discussion, refuted the attorney for the outside directors. It said that on September 18, 1985, the special committee convened by the outside directors unanimously had approved a resolution declaring that "it was the sense of the Board" that "it was inappropriate and not in the best interests of Macy for the management directors to seek to purchase Macy by procedures initiated and directed by them and that accordingly the management directors were directed not to proceed at that time." The resolution instructed the committee "to consider all appropriate ways of maximizing shareholder values, including the possibility of a buyout of Macy." Later that day, the full board adopted the special committee's report.

But Tanenbaum persisted.

"Why isn't there as much opportunity for management to give itself stock in a public company as there would be in a private company?" he asked. Then, pointing a finger at the chairman, the attorney said, "You, Mr. Finkelstein, will be getting a large share of the new company for almost nothing." Reading from the proxy statement, Tanenbaum said that the Macy chief would get $9.75 million for his Macy stock and stock options and would pay only $4.37 million for about 25 percent of the stock in the new company.

During Tanenbaum's angry oration, Finkelstein had listened with some patient exasperation but without interjecting any comment, until the other man finished. "I must register strong disagreement with you," Finkelstein finally said.

And for the next few minutes, he read some prepared remarks for the shareholders. It was, of course, entirely tailored to the audience and to the occasion and had some of the sonority of a swan song for a company about to go private.

"R. H. Macy became a company known for its formidable undertakings and impressive successes, though, over the years, the company had its ups and downs," Finkelstein said. "During the last decade or so, Macy's has emerged as the nation's premier retailer, an innovator, a leader in financial performance. Our emergence as an industry leader has been marked by our ability to predict and respond to retailing trends, coupled with our willingness to blaze new paths, to reach out in new directions.

"Macy's shareholders supported our growth and development since we first went public in 1922. We are grateful for the support our shareholders have provided over those years. Now we have reached another milestone in our history. We have made the determination that Macy's should return to being a private company. We believe that as a private company, Macy's can implement the long-term strategies and planning necessary to respond to current trends in this fast-moving economic environment and so serve our customers better."

He told the shareholders that management was certain that the pending transaction would enhance Macy's ability "to continue to be a forceful and competitive retailer. I need hardly remind you that two major New York stores, Gimbels and Ohrbach's, have just announced that they will close. They thus join the long list of retail failures in the New York community. And you can take it as fact that the pace of retail competition is no less hectic every place where Macy's operates."

Finkelstein said that he and his colleagues were convinced that to succeed in such a highly competitive business, Macy's had to continue to attract and train the best people and keep them. "Losing important executives sets back or defeats the best-laid plans," he said. "The fact is that it is because of our Macy people that we have done so well. That's why we've structured this transaction in a way that permits participation by an unprecedented number of people within our organization. And we've provided the opportunity for future 'stars' to participate as well. We believe in ownership as an incentive to superior performance. That's why we have created this unique transaction.

"We are confident that we are doing this in a way that serves the best interests of everyone connected with Macy's," Finkelstein continued.

"Shareholders will receive fair value for their investment. Our key people will have the opportunity to invest in the enterprise of which they are an integral part. Our customers will continue to enjoy excellent service and merchandise. And by running a vibrant business, we can also serve our other constituencies as well—our vendors, our vital employee group, the communities of which we are a part.

"My colleagues and I thank you all for your support over the years," he said. "We want you to know that it has been our pleasure to serve you." And, in his final remark concerning the buyout proposal, he said that "the financing is essentially in place. Everyone is hard at work, and I anticipate a closing by the end of the month." He added, "By the way, we are not having our usual stockholders' sandwich luncheon this time, due to the present circumstances."

There was silence, scattered applause, then silence again. The decision not to provide the simple luncheon, which would have represented a touch of nicety at a sensitive time, did not surprise those in the room who knew Finkelstein well. He could be very sensitive at an opportune moment and very insensitive at the worst possible one. And if anyone felt that he or she was being closed out as a shareholder while all "other constituencies" were being taken care of, it was almost too late. Obviously, a vote was soon to be taken on the buyout proposal. But Tanenbaum rose once again, doggedly repeating some of his earlier charges.

The meeting had lasted for more than an hour—Finkelstein felt worn and annoyed and he showed it. "You are totally incorrect," he told Tanenbaum, "that I am getting my interest for nothing. Besides my own investment, I am taking the risk."

Charging that Finkelstein and his board members had failed to fulfill their fiduciary responsibilities to the shareholders, Tanenbaum once shot to his feet and declared, "What we need is some court action! Who will join me to organize a group to fight this thing in the courts? I invite anyone interested to meet me now in the back of the auditorium!"

About eight of the five hundred or so shareholders joined Tanenbaum in the rear, where they noisily milled about as Macy clericals distributed cards for a vote on the buyout. Tanenbaum was heard angrily talking among his handful of cohorts as the votes were tallied. The motion was approved overwhelmingly—40,452,583 votes in favor, or 78.33 of the total 51.2 million outstanding common shares. Opposed were only 885,801 votes, or 1.71 percent. It was, in short, a rout. Finkelstein had his buyout.

CHAPTER TWO

MACY'S AND
ITS MERCHANTS

Macy's was New York, as much a symbol, a source of pride, and an identifying landmark to New Yorkers as the Empire State Building, Yankee Stadium, Central Park, Radio City Music Hall, or the Brooklyn Bridge. Viewing the gray, towering rise of the sixteen-story, block-square Herald Square store, New Yorkers thought it only natural that the building should bear the proclamation "The World's Largest Store"; that its policy for years, "6 Percent Less for Cash," was what they deserved; that its mammoth July Fourth fireworks extravaganza over the Hudson River and the famous, nationally televised Thanksgiving Day parade were tokens of Macy's esteem for its millions of loyal customers. It was all a love affair between the giant department store and generations of customers.

And tourists, domestic or foreign, could only agree, as they listened to their proud, resident relatives or others eager to tell them what the edifice really was. New York was grand, glorious, unique. And so, by implication, was Macy's.

But what they could hardly have known, natives and visitors alike, was that the giant store had been struggling for years. Although Macy had been a public company since 1922, the company did not break down results of its divisions in its reports to shareholders. No one on the outside therefore really knew how well the flagship store, the other fourteen stores in the New York division, or for that matter the other divisions in New Jersey, Atlanta, Kansas City, or San Francisco, were doing. But enough inside information was leaking out so that the difficulties of the 2.1-million-square-foot behemoth were becoming apparent. Its profits were intermittent, up one year, down the second, entirely missing the third. But it wasn't just the reputation of the main store that was hurt. It was the whole New York division, for as the Herald Square store went so did the fourteen others. Though it was only one of the five Macy store divisions, the Manhattan-based one was the jewel of the cluster, setting the tone and the glow.

Oddly enough, the moderate profits of the total R. H. Macy didn't seem to bother those people who knew. Macy's was Macy's, the paragon, the battlewagon of America's department store industry, probably the most famous retailer in the country. No matter that others, such as Federated Department Stores, the May Department Stores Company, or Mercantile Stores, had fatter profits or more dynamic managements in the decades from the end of World War II through the 1974–75 recession. In those years and before, Macy's commanded everyone's respect and affection, a dowager queen even if her robes were frayed, her eyesight somewhat deprived.

Many had occupied those managers' offices on the thirteenth floor over the years. Some were talented, some impressive, some inept. Almost all continued to observe the tradition that changes were to be limited, evolutionary, and basically only refinements on an already well-defined strategy. Dignity and integrity—personified by the occasional, fierce admonitions of Jack I. Straus as family patriarch, resident leader, and spokesman—were to be upheld.

"Mr. Jack," as many respectful employees addressed him, loved to pose for press photographers on the mezzanine of the Herald Square store so that even a relatively narrow lens could capture the mass of shoppers on the main floor below. The patent attempt to dramatize the pull of "the world's largest store" was usually softened by the demeanor of a calm, unsmiling, dignified man. "Mr. Jack's" frown could chill, but his smile always seemed to imbue its beneficiary with the proud tradition of Macy's. Sitting in his office or walking the aisles of the floor in a dark suit, rep tie, and with triangular tip of white handkerchief showing, "Mr. Jack" always preserved the role of family owner long after the Straus family had sold almost all their holdings in the 1920s. It appeared to be his right and no one in those years would dare to think otherwise. The lean, bespectacled Jack Straus came from hardy, entrepreneurial forebears who had left an indelible stamp on New York.

Macy's should really have been called "Macy and Straus," considering that Jack Straus's great-grandfather, Lazarus Straus, became associated with Rowland H. Macy as long ago as 1874. Sixteen years earlier, in 1858, the Nantucket Quaker whaling man opened his fifth and ultimately his only successful dry goods shop in Manhattan. The store with the eleven-foot front on Sixth Avenue near Fourteenth Street seemed only destined to fail, as had Rowland Macy's two shops in Boston, one in Haverhill, Massachusetts, and another in Marysville, California. But he had learned some basic storekeeping principles along the way—buying strictly for cash, selling strictly for cash, and adhering strictly to one price—that found favor with New Yorkers and other residents of the nearby area. He also benefited from the fact that the typical urban customer's requirements had grown so in number and sophistication that the peddlers and other dry goods stores of the day were proving to be inadequate. He was canny enough to realize that he had to add new lines of merchandise to keep customers interested and returning often. His new store was also on a main traffic street. Good location and merchandise excitement, a combination that later merchants were to stubbornly claim as their own discovery, was Rowland Hussey Macy's secret a century earlier.

Macy's first day's receipts of $11.06 hardly dented his enthusiasm. His earlier cross-country wandering and the time he spent on the seas seemed to fill him with a zest for adventure in his mercantile career. Constantly, he tested the risk of a token, new line—men's hosiery and ties, then linens and towels, then European "fancy" goods, then costume jewelry, then silver and clocks—and when the invigorated tastes of New Yorkers and tourists took to it, he expanded each so that by 1870 his store had become almost complete in its merchandise array. It was also the year when his sales scaled the $1 million level.

To this day, the Macy family might conceivably have continued to own the store if it hadn't been for Rowland Macy's lack of faith in his own son, R. H. Macy, Jr. His solution to the problem of succession began inadvertently in 1860, only two years after he had opened his doors, when he hired Margaret Getchell, a pert Nantucket schoolteacher, to be his bookkeeper. Perhaps instinctively, he employed her in the realization that a woman might be very useful in a business where most of the customers were women. The fact that Margaret was a distant relative no doubt helped to shore up his faith in her.

Because of that relationship, he sympathized with her when he found that she had taken to Abiel T. LaForge, a handsome, young salesman. LaForge was given a job at Macy's and soon after married Margaret. For a while, Macy even allowed them to live in a tiny apartment above the store. Promoted by the affectionate Macy, the former salesman received increasing responsibility in the growing business. And when the founder viewed his son's lack of interest in the store, he singled out LaForge and Robert M. Valentine, Macy's nephew, to be his business heirs.

When Rowland Macy died suddenly in 1877 while on a buying trip in France, the two acquired his store, but LaForge's good fortune ran out. Soon after, he contracted tuberculosis and died. Valentine, after buying LaForge's share, attempted to keep the business within Macy family hands by bringing in as LaForge's successor Charles Webster, a relative and co-worker, but the succession line thinned further. When Valentine died, Webster loyally married the widow and brought in his brother-in-law, Jerome B. Wheeler. In 1887, a decade after Rowland Macy's death, Webster and Wheeler parted company with Webster buying him out. But Webster realized that despite his decade's experience in operating Macy's, he lacked two major ingredients: broader retailing knowledge and a strong, sure hand at the controls of the business.

Enter the Strauses.

Lazarus Straus, a liberal-minded, German-Jewish businessman, emigrated to the United States in 1852, disillusioned over the collapse of the 1848 revolution in Germany, which had sought to democratize that country's rigid, monarchic society. At forty-three, starting over not with a business in the populated Eastern Seaboard of the U.S. but with a small general store in Talbotton, Georgia, he established an American business dynasty. Leon Harris, himself a member of such a productive family, said in his 1979 book, *Merchant Princes*: "The only Jewish merchant family in America that approximates the Rothschilds in Europe is the Straus family. They have been the only family—with the exception of the Rosenwalds—to amass a great fortune and to create a style of life as notable as the Rothschilds' in terms of luxury, of generosity and of service."

Before he opened his new store, Lazarus traveled the roads and small towns as a peddler. It was not an unusual vocation for immigrants in the middle and late decades of the nineteenth century. Adam Gimbel carried a pack and peddled in a wagon up and down the Mississippi before opening a store in Vincennes, Indiana. David May peddled and then became a miner before he established a store in Leadville, Colorado. After working in his two brothers' store in Downieville, California, Aaron Meier went out on many peddling trips in the Oregon Territory before Portland, a town of about two thousand, attracted his interest and he opened a store there. With such paltry beginnings, these three seeded the immense retail chains: Gimbel Brothers, May Department Stores Company, and Meier & Frank.

Two years after he arrived in the tiny southern town, Lazarus Straus brought over his wife, Sara, and their four children. Lazarus was then forty-five, a stern, upright man who sorely missed his father, Jacob Ben Lazar, who had remained behind. He believed strongly in the work ethic for his three sons, Isidor, Nathan, and Oscar, and his daughter, Hermina, and in a tight family budget. The children worked in the store, which remained open until 9:30 in the evening, helping to serve customers, cleaning, and studying by the illumination of kerosene lamps when shopping slowed. At home, they assisted Sara and also tended to the garden.

Sara, who also helped in the store, says Leon Harris in his book, received "a monthly allowance of $20, from which she was able to save something even after buying a piano for Hermina. . . . Their occasional luxuries were made possible by constant thrift."

During the Civil War, Lazarus and Isidor, the oldest son, were loyal, even zealous Confederates—both bought and traded in Confederate bonds, hoping to raise funds for the South. Isidor traveled through Europe to sell bonds to England, Germany, and France, where he also tried to arrange for ships from those and other countries to break the Yankee sea blockade that was so damaging to the Confederate cause. He also sought to bring much-needed arms.

When the depleted South threw down its weapons, Lazarus and Sara decided that the family would fare better in the North. Isidor had managed to save about $10,000 worth of gold and bought the family a house in Manhattan, where the Strauses moved in 1867. Lazarus purchased a wholesale chinaware-importing firm, which he renamed L. Straus and Sons and brought his sons into it. Seven years later, seeing a better potential in retail selling, the Strauses leased twenty-five hundred square feet of space in Macy's, one of the principal stores that they had supplied with their china, glassware, and silver.

Taking note of their success and growing contribution to the store's business, Charles Webster, in 1887, eagerly offered the Strauses a partnership. Their sales had already grown to almost 20 percent of the store's total and the department was its most profitable. There was no doubt in Webster's mind that the Strauses would make ideal partners. Under the new partnership, Webster and the Strauses briskly matched and undercut the prices of their major rivals such as A. T. Stewart, Hearn's, and Siegel & Cooper. It proved a sound policy. That first full year of the new partnership, Macy's sales rose to an unprecedented $5 million, and business grew at a steady annual 10 percent after that.

Wisely, Webster let the Strauses indulge their creative bent. They led all the others in establishing the odd-price policy, $4.98 instead of $5, which prompted economical housewives to feel that these shavings off the price added up to bargains if they bought a number of items. Taking a leaf from the adventurous style of the founder, the Strauses continuously added to the merchandise Macy sold—Oriental rugs, ornate bedsteads, engraved stationery, bicycles, pianos—convincing shoppers that Macy's had everything for everyone. They influenced their partner to accommodate shoppers who turned up without much cash so that they could buy through "Depositors' Accounts." Those customers could make deposits and charge purchases against those sums. It was a progenitor of the later "layaway" plan and, more important, of the eventual widespread installment buying that was to astronomically build everyone's retail business. It was a shrewd ploy, not just in terms of producing more Macy's business, it also allowed the owners to amass funds at no interest from the pockets of its shoppers.

Meanwhile, in Brooklyn in 1868, another young merchant, Abraham Abraham, had started a tiny shop with a partner, Joseph Wechsler. A feisty, hyperenergetic young man, Abraham previously had been a salesclerk at the Bettlebeck & Company store in Newark, across the Hudson, where he had worked alongside two other young salesmen, Lyman Bloomingdale and Benjamin Altman. All three were later to found their own great department stores in New York, but at the time, Abraham had other ambitions. Fired by the Union cause during the Civil War, he shocked his staid parents by suddenly leaving home to enlist against the Confederacy. He felt that Chicago, far from home, would be the proper place to do so, but his parents found him there and forced the eighteen-year-old to return home.

His energy now turned toward his little shop. If Brooklyn as an outpost of New York ever dismayed the two founders of Abraham & Wechsler, the planned opening of the great Brooklyn Bridge inspired them. Timing their entry into a newer, larger store to coincide with the unveiling of the bridge, they proudly awaited customers in a five-story store at 420 Fulton Street. But the novelty wore off for Wechsler, and in 1893 he found others to buy his interest. For $1.5 million, Isidor and Nathan Straus (Lazarus had died in 1888) and Charles Webster became the half owners of the Brooklyn store. Abraham & Straus—the store's new name—remained a separate business from Macy's, but Isidor Straus, while carefully watching Macy's finances, was a constant critic of Abraham Abraham. The Brooklyn merchant responded to Straus's polite scolding by shoring up his executive staff with his own family members. Despite the rift, both Macy's and A&S thrived as independent businesses in their own boroughs, learning from each other as they grew to dominate New York's retail market.

One can only speculate as to why the Strauses thought it more proper to rename Abraham & Wechsler, Abraham & Straus but not R. H. Macy & Company, Macy & Straus. Of course, it made no sense at all to do both. Probably the main reason they renamed the Brooklyn store to include their name was that it wasn't as well known or entrenched as Macy's. Changing the Abraham & Wechsler name wouldn't hurt, they probably reasoned, and it didn't make much sense to retain the Wechsler name as an appendage to the more familiar "Abraham" when the original partnership had ended.

But the insertion of the Straus name also meant something else. At a time when great pioneering merchants such as Alexander T. Stewart, John Wanamaker, and Rowland Macy strode across the New York–Philadelphia scene or had already left their mark, the Straus family, which owned a substantial part of two of the area's biggest department stores went unheralded. It was a singular triumph for the descendants of Lazarus Straus that a major store finally bore the family name.

In 1896, eight years after he invited the Strauses into Macy's, Charles Webster sold his half interest to them, permanently ending the ownership of the one family and allowing it to pass to another. In 1902, Lazarus Straus's sons stood proudly as they unveiled "The World's Largest Store" at Thirty-fourth Street and Broadway. It was another tribute to their visionary father, a fact that the oldest son, Isidor, made certain to observe to his own children, Jesse, Percy, and Herbert, who were already in the business, too.

But he didn't need to motivate them to recognize their family obligations, nor, indeed, to spur them to any more zeal in following his and Lazarus's ambition. The three young men had already shown it by urging Isidor to move uptown to the Thirty-fourth Street site. It didn't matter one bit—in fact, it was an intriguing commentary on how economic opportunities never lay too far away from man's basic instincts—that the giant new store would be directly across the street from the city's two most famous brothels, the Tivoli and the Pekin.

The cost of the new store was huge, $4.5 million, which the family was easily able to borrow because of the success of Macy's, not to mention the growth of their "other" store over the Brooklyn Bridge. The Strauses didn't even need to offer either store and its inventory as collateral because their credit standing was high among the big New York banks. Lazarus Straus was one of the very few southern business-men who had honored his debts to all his northern suppliers after the war had ended, and that integrity had become the core of the family's excellent credit rating years later.

But there was one problem with the Thirty-fourth Street site: they couldn't have all of it, particularly the strategic corner tip at Thirty-fourth Street and Broadway. Another merchant had outwitted them by capturing it and he sought to use it to his strategic advantage. As Tom Mahoney and Leonard Sloane tell it in their 1966 book, *The Great Merchants:*

> The choice of Macy's present location at Thirty-fourth Street and Broad-way, a crossroads which has gained in importance over the years, was at the time a radical leapfrog over the competition in the movement of New York retailing. It was particularly alarming to Henry Siegel, a Chicago merchant who had just pushed the center of shopping gravity northward by building Siegel Cooper New York on Eighteenth Street. Through agents, Siegel bought up a little over a thousand square feet of the Thirty-fourth Street and Broadway corner, paying $375,000 for it. Then he offered it to the Strauses for only $250,000 if they would sell him the unexpired lease on their old Fourteenth Street store and with it the custom of shoppers used to the location.
>
> The Strauses refused to pay tribute. They instructed their architects to build around the little corner—which is still, incidentally, unoccupied by Macy's—and used the $250,000 they had ear-marked for its acquisi-tion to acquire land to the west, on which a twenty-story building was erected in 1924.

(That tiny corner, by the way, has been occupied for years by a Nedick's fast-food shop, a garish blip on Macy's frontal exposure which has annoyed Macyites for a long time.)

The new Macy quickly became a draw for New Yorkers and tourists, a vast emporium that with A. T. Stewart's store only a few miles away on Astor Place became the premier department store in America, striking a path that many others followed.

The Herald Square store was the only department store of its time to install pneumatic tubes to move cash or messages; the first to establish a vacuum system to rid the store of stale air and odors; and the first to install modern escalators with flat steps, replacing the earlier ones with wedges for the shopper's feet. It was also the first store large enough to provide room to adequately service the shopper, with a full complement of fitting rooms, accommodation desks, an information counter, and a sufficient number of rest rooms. Because of its opening "one-price" policy and its odd-pricing practice, Macy's customers were zealous in notifying management where there seemed to be a mistake or lack of competitive pricing by Macy's. As a result, the management hired a group of clerks to monitor the competition, checking the others' prices and giving rise to the comparison-shopping practice later adopted by almost the entire industry. Success seemed to follow every new addition or installation that the Strauses made. That first year of the Herald Square store's existence, sales boomed to almost $11 million, having more than doubled in four years.

After Lazarus Straus's death, Isidor Straus had comfortably slipped into the role of family head. He had always had a deep family sense, shown even as a very young man when he had bought the home for his parents in New York. But while he involved himself in everything in both stores, he was less known to the public than his extroverted, younger brother, Nathan. The younger Straus lacked Isidor's dignity, but he was popular among the employees and peers in New York business. He walked along the aisles at Macy whistling popular songs and often spoke to clerks and customers. Isidor, too, frequently showed himself on the sales floor, but while Nathan was natty in his grooming, Isidor was formal and rather forbidding. He always wore a high hat, frock coat, and high wing collar as he strode along the selling floor. Nathan also presented himself more outside the store than Isidor, appearing often at the race track, sometimes involving himself in city politics and becoming an eager, free-handed philanthropist. His interest in charitable endeavors brought him such satisfaction and fame that in 1914 he resigned from Macy's and for the better part of the next two decades in which he lived gave away the bulk of his fortune.

After obtaining a law degree, Oscar, the youngest of Lazarus's sons, had entered the political world and backed the candidacy of President

Grover Cleveland, who rewarded him with the ambassadorial post to Turkey. The selection of a Jew proved controversial, but Cleveland wasn't swayed by the pressure. Charming, clever, and honest, Oscar later drew considerable praise for his work in Turkey, particularly in mediating a dispute involving European railway interests and the Ottoman empire. In 1906, President Theodore Roosevelt took the unprecedented step of appointing Oscar Straus to his cabinet as secretary of commerce and labor. The protests rose once more but then and afterward Roosevelt defended his appointment of the first Jew in a presidential cabinet as nothing more or less than a well-merited choice.

Isidor's fame, however, endured longer than either of his two brothers'. The reason was a combination of tragedy and courage. In April 1912, Isidor and Ida, his wife, embarked on the maiden voyage of the *Titanic* to New York. Milling around the deck with them were other wealthy Americans, people bearing the names of Widener, Astor, Guggenheim. On April 15, as the immense, shining White Star ship plowed through the swells in an overcast sky, it collided with an iceberg and in less than three hours began going down. Isidor, always proud but reserved, stubbornly refused to enter a lifeboat. It was clear to all that even with the admonition that "women and children first" be saved, there weren't enough lifeboats for all. He urged Ida to save herself. Her reply was simple. Having been married to Isidor for forty years, she said, she wouldn't end it at that moment.

Afterward, the distraught family installed a plaque to Isidor's and Ida's selfless courage in the store that remains to face all visitors to the thirteenth floor. The children, the three sons and the three daughters, also established Straus Hall at Harvard University and contributed numerous other gifts there in their parents' memory.

Then, as in any family business when the patriarch passes on, the question of succession and ownership arose. But, in the case of the Strauses, it was complicated by a combination of generational differences and sibling rivalries. Although Isidor had exhorted his sons, Jesse, Percy, and Herbert, to honor Nathan's wishes and dictates as much as they did his own, the three did not get along well with Nathan. This was partly because of his growing interests away from the store and also because they knew he resented the fact that his older brother's sons had received more responsibility in the business than had his own. What rankled Nathan, too, was the knowledge that his nephews were more talented and interested in the company than his two sons were. He was torn between disappointment in them and pride in his nephews.

The decision that the situation dictated was clear enough. Nathan owned half of the business and Isidor's sons the other half. Oscar had long since disposed of his interest to the other family members. The two factions didn't even seriously contemplate a joint ownership. What was the best solution to the problem? One group would simply have to sell to the other. Jesse, Percy, and Herbert, after conferring with their counsel, suggested that a figure of $7 million was proper for either a sale of their holdings to Nathan and his family or for a sale of his interest to them. Nathan then made his counteroffer. He would sell his share if they would throw in as partial payment their half ownership of Abraham & Straus, as well as their interest in the wholesale china-glassware company that the family had kept up after acquiring Macy's. Jesse, Percy, and Herbert accepted and became the sole owners of Macy's.

Jesse and Percy had for some time been taking full responsibility for the store and they fell naturally into their new role. Jesse, who assumed the primary post, was not eager to change policies or prac-tices from those followed by his father. Despite Isidor's strict upbring-ing of his three sons, especially of Jesse, the oldest, they had adored the stern parent. More than the other sons or daughters, Jesse had taken to the atmosphere of the brilliant, busy establishment. When the time arrived for him to go to college, he wanted to work at Macy's instead. But Isidor insisted that he matriculate first at Harvard. Even after he graduated, Isidor didn't want him in the store until he had gathered several years' experience, first working as a clerk in a New York bank. Finally, after a year and a half, the father relented and allowed him to take a salesman's job at Abraham & Straus. Three years after leaving Harvard, Jesse was permitted to join Macy's.

So great was the son's devotion to Isidor that Jesse after his father's death wanted only to be called formally, "Jesse Isidor." And he gave his own son, Jack, the same middle name.

This tightly knit relationship also marked the manner in which both Jesse and Percy, his younger brother, assumed their responsibilities in the family business. They were formally "Mr. Jesse" and "Mr. Percy" to employees and other businessmen, and they were so close and already so entrenched in running the massive store that the youngest brother, Herbert, remained a less active third member of the team. When a major decision or issue arose, the two older Strauses would close their doors to the others, calmly discuss the matter and then one would open the door to announce, "My brother [or brothers] and I have decided that what we shall do . . ." When someone would demand why they had taken that position, as often as not Jesse would respond, "Poppa would have done the same."

Much was said decades later, particularly in the 1950s and 1960s, about the discounters' fight with nationally branded producers over fixed prices. But Jesse and Percy persisted in underselling any brands that they could and it was only a matter of time before retribution would descend upon them. Oddly enough, it wasn't a major household product that did it but books that Macy sold at 20 percent to 25 percent below the publisher's advertised price. In 1909, a book publishers' association sued Macy, charging that the price-cutting hurt the true value of their copyright. The Strauses, contending that the group represented an illegal trust under the Sherman Antitrust Act, counter-sued. The publishers responded by completely cutting off supply. But Macy, presaging the later discounters' practice of buying goods through transshippers, wholesalers, or other retailers who overbought in the traditional channels just to reship to banned channels, was able to obtain many titles over the years, even from authors, who privately sold Macy's their copies. The litigation went on and on until 1913, when the U.S. Supreme Court rendered a decision backing Macy. But even then, and since, when Macy wanted well-known brands to sell at discounts, branded suppliers found ways to make it difficult. And it was one major spur to the store's management to build its own brands, variously called "private labels" or "store labels," to give it the pricing independence, and not so incidentally the better markups the Strauses and their later hired professional managers craved.

After the war ended in 1918, Macy's annual volume amounted to about $36 million, double its 1914 sales. The cash reserves mounted and its credit lines grew, so for the first time the Strauses began thinking of opening in other cities. In 1923, they acquired the LaSalle & Koch stores in Toledo and in 1924 the Davison-Paxon department store in Atlanta. Just before the Depression, they made what became their most astute acquisition by buying L. Bamberger & Company, of Newark, New Jersey. The moves gave Macy's toeholds in three other cities and later, in the 1940s, they were also to add existing stores in San Francisco and Kansas City, Missouri. In three decades, Macy had leaped across the country, becoming the nation's biggest department store chain.

In those first years of expansion, Jesse I. Straus assumed not only a principal role as great merchant but his constantly growing fortune and prominence inevitably drew him into politics. In 1931, the handsome, tall, elegantly groomed Straus was selected by New York governor Franklin Delano Roosevelt to head the state's temporary emergency relief effort to aid the unemployed. A conservative Democrat, he was one of the few American businessmen the following year to support Roosevelt for the presidency. After the victory, there seemed to be reason to expect Jesse Straus to follow his uncle, Oscar, into the president's cabinet. But Roosevelt instead named Straus as his ambassador to France.

The Straus grandsons followed their forebears into the business, and Jack I. Straus, Jesse's son, became chairman of R. H. Macy in 1940. More than any of his cousins, he had the benefit of not only being literally raised in retailing—he had wielded the silver trowel as a two-year-old at the Herald Square opening in 1902—but also of hearing his father and his uncle, Percy, at the breakfast table heatedly discussing store matters. If they thought he was too young to be absorbing anything, they were wrong. He grew up on a business religion that customers wanted just what Macy had always counted on—lots of diverse merchandise of good quality and attentive salespeople and store executives who weren't too busy to give the customer the full attention she deserved. If later this proved not to be the case at Macy's, it wasn't because "Mr. Jack" was responsible. He may have earned a minor reputation as an enthusiastic amateur jazz pianist but he was a disciplinarian in the store.

Tall, very thin, and reserved, more like his grandfather, Isidor, and his great-grandfather, Lazarus, than his own father, Jesse, Jack Straus found that he had to promote professionals up through the ranks as his top executives. His own son, Kenneth, became a merchandising vice-president and Jack's two cousins, Edward and John, the sons of Herbert Straus, held major posts in the organization, but not in the top suite. It became uncomfortably apparent to "Mr. Jack" that the family tree, always so fruitful for the better part of a century, was becoming bare of the strong limbs vitally needed to sustain Macy's growth.

Those professionals who came to sit in offices near Straus's own on the thirteenth floor and to head the four other divisions were a diverse group. Most started in Macy's famous executive training squad, where they spent several months in both classroom and on-the-job training in various departments. Ernest L. Molloy, who had been raised in the Boston suburb of Cambridge, joined the squad in 1929 after graduation from Harvard. After a series of executive jobs, he became chairman of the San Francisco division, where he stayed more than a dozen years until "Mr. Jack" tapped him for the corporate presidency in the mid-sixties because he respected Molloy's merchandising instincts and wanted another disciplined executive, preferably a merchant, to join him at the top executive level.

Herbert L. Seegal, who occupied both the presidency of the Macy New York and Bamberger's divisions, was one of the few outsiders hired by Jack Straus for a major post. Seegal, also a Bostonian, was one of the top merchandising executives at Thalhimer Brothers, a department store chain in Richmond, Virginia, when Straus decided he needed a fashion merchant in the New York division. His move to Macy proved to be one of the most important additions ever made to its executive team. An introverted, intellectual, and extremely insightful man, Seegal had a merchandising intellect that cut through tradition and red tape. He pioneered the concept of full inventories, even deliberately inflated in case there were unexpected sales surges, and especially pushed the full-stock, high-service quotient for branch stores. They were not to be considered branches because that denigrated their importance within the organization. Each store was to be considered as important as any other, branches as much as divisional flagships.

Donald B. Smiley, a financial man in the New York division, became a particular favorite of "Mr. Jack" for his cool approach to the demands that merchandising made on the balance sheet. That is not to say that he looked down his nose at the merchandise aspect, but he was able to demonstrate to the chairman that he could not be unduly swayed by perspiring, overenthusiastic merchants. Straus made Smiley corporate vice-chairman and he eventually succeeded "Mr. Jack" in the top corporate job, functioning in a tandem management with Herb Seegal as president.

David L. Yunich, an upstate New York native, was a graduate of the training squad, after playing semiprofessional baseball in Syracuse while attending Union College. After completing Harvard Graduate School of Business, his rise at Macy was fast, a buyer within one year and a vice-president within three. Chunky, charismatic, bandy-legged like the baseball catcher that he was, Yunich had the easy, informal, confident manner of the ball field, and he built friendships up and down the executive line that lasted for years. Like Seegal, whose career at Macy he duplicated in many ways, although the two never warmed to each other, Yunich became president of Bamberger's and then of Macy's New York. He and Seegal were two entirely different personalities, Seegal a professional scholar of retailing who preferred to be a loner among the executive team, Yunich a highly skilled merchant and gifted administrator whose smile and backslapping manner easily broke many barriers. But, as he told me with a rueful smile, "I was always referred to as a good administrator, but I would have preferred to be known as a good merchant. That's what brought me into this business." Yunich created the new policy in which store buyers were separated from their selling floor responsibilities and sales training role to concentrate on their buying function. It was a seminal change that was widely adopted in the industry. And it was during his administration at Macy's New York in the mid-sixties that the New York division unveiled its famous "store-in-the-round" in the Elmhurst section of Queens, New York. Essentially a square store built into a Colosseum-like round structure, with twin, circular parking decks, it was a startling innovation and drew considerable pro-and-con debate in the city and in the industry.

There were other executives, too, particularly in the store divisions, but with one exception none rose to the stellar heights of the big offices on the thirteenth floor in Herald Square. The only man who did was Edward S. Finkelstein, the son of a butter-and-egg merchant in New Rochelle, New York, who came to Macy's training squad in 1948 and emerged as the most important, innovative, and controversial executive in many years.

CHAPTER THREE

HARVARD, HERALD
SQUARE, AND NEWARK

Ed Finkelstein graduated from the Harvard Graduate School of Business in 1948, the year before the often-heralded 1949 class of stars which included his eventual, strongest rival, Marvin S. Traub, the chairman and chief executive officer of Bloomingdale's.

In those academic years from 1941 through 1948, as a Harvard undergraduate and as a graduate student, classmates recall the young Finkelstein as a leaner, less certain, more somber man than he was in later years. His determination impressed those classmates but frequently he showed that he wasn't clear about the future role he wanted to pursue.

His career confusion was not uncommon among young men, however able. A fine student, he was certain that there must be an intellectual challenge and considerable personal excitement in climbing up in the business world, although he knew that it wasn't a noble calling, as he said much later, "like being called into the priesthood or medicine or the law." Yet he chose to major in economics—partly because his father was in business—and applied himself, eventually graduating cum laude.

There was another reason for his choice. Although his father, Maurice, had a successful butter-and-egg business in Westchester County, New York, allowing the family to live comfortably, Ed couldn't help but be impressed by many of the sumptuous homes he saw in the nearby towns of Scarsdale, Harrison, and Larchmont. His parents' home in New Rochelle was very modest by comparison and it was hard not to envy the wealth and the power of the many families in the area, the bedroom community of New York City, and wonder what his own life might produce.

He was born March 30, 1925, to Maurice Finkelstein and the former Eva Levine. At seventeen, he graduated from Mount Vernon High School, a precocious student, and he was offered scholarships to two universities. But he had learned a couple of vital things. The business career he had decided upon seemed right for him, for his particular talents. He could quickly absorb facts and he also had a facility to see their significance or the lack of it. Those primary assets had already carried him close to the top of his high school class. The other thing he knew was that a degree from the finest American college, Harvard, would be indispensable to edging his way up through the marketplace. After all, if a company was the biggest and the best, it would seek applicants from the premier educational institutions.

Spurning the scholarships, he borrowed money from an uncle, applied to Harvard, and was accepted into the class of 1942. That first year, he waited on tables to finance his tuition. In the second year, he joined the Navy's V-12 program for college students. As a result, he technically served in the Navy while attending school through 1946, when he graduated and was discharged from the armed services. He enrolled in the Harvard graduate school and by the graduation year of 1948, he had become indoctrinated in the school's classic case-study method. It taught him the value of a traditional approach to management principles with a core of balance, structure, and entrepreneurism.

While at the graduate school, he came under the influence of Malcolm McNair, the Lincoln Filene professor of retailing, the nation's leading academic guru of that business discipline, whose encyclopedic knowledge, gently tart tongue, and sense of retailing cycles allowed him to impart a pragmatic wisdom to his students. Later, Finkelstein became exposed to another business sage, Peter Drucker, who eventually became his great mentor. Ed devoted himself to reading every one of Drucker's many books and professed that he had based his career on that scholar's monumental works, which included an accurate prediction of the ups and downs of Sears, Roebuck and Company, the world's largest retailer. Drucker was also an admirer of Marks & Spencer, the giant British retail concern, which while copying some of Sears's methods, notably in recruiting, training, and developing new executives, was imbued with a variety of objectives, perhaps more diverse than Sears's, productivity and marketing, for example. It had also established "innovation objectives," as Drucker put it, by which "it rapidly built its quality-control laboratories into research, design and development centers. It developed designs and fashions. Finally, it went out and looked for the right manufacturer." The result was one of the world's best programs for private labels, in particular, St. Michael's. It was to become a subject of great interest to Finkelstein and was reflected in some of his own innovations at Macy.

By the time he received his M.B.A., Finkelstein had also narrowed down his specialty. It would be either retailing or marketing, and when R. H. Macy offered him a spot on its executive training squad, the new graduate promptly accepted. After the requisite months in the classroom and on-the-job training, he was promoted to buyer of fabrics. It wasn't a choice job, but it was a rapid recognition of his ability to accept responsibility. The fabric business, despite Macy's relatively big department and loyal home-sewing clientele, was a very basic one. But the market was beginning to respond to some innovation, reflecting the revived interest in women's fashions. Paris couture was coming to life again, and its stimulus was filtering across the ocean and into various categories of merchandise. If whites and some prints had been their mainstay, the fabric sections of Macy's, Bloomingdale's, and Gimbels were also beginning to show pink, yellow, mauve, and other colors, as well as new larger prints, florals, and patterns. The shift improved the fabric department's traditionally low turnover rate, but it was a slow evolution. The explosion of designer names and abstracts and daring imports were still some light-years away. It was not an environment to greatly excite an ambitious, upwardly mobile young man.

But he did well, and within just a few years was promoted to merchandise administrator, Macy's definition for divisional merchandise manager. Now he supervised other buyers. It was his first important experience in managing people, although as a buyer he had worked with salespeople. This, however, was different, because the efforts of the buyers would directly affect his performance and that of Macy. The challenge of working through other executives was an enjoyable, thrilling prospect. And he soon learned that he couldn't behave as a puppet master, it couldn't be a matter of jerking anyone on a string. You had to sell them on the value of certain operating and marketing principles while convincing them that their intrinsic responsibility had to be more entrepreneurial than functionary. It was a simple matter of teaching, always teaching, with a prod now and then.

Although he commuted every day from Westchester County and hadn't prior to matriculating at Cambridge traveled farther from home than to visit his Aunt Jenny in New Jersey, by the early 1960s he had evolved into a big-city, big-business type. He had also evolved into a trim, dark-haired young man with tight cheekbones, a husky, determined voice, and a soft, cultured manner. If there was one trait that emerged from the Finkelstein persona, it was perhaps earnestness. Good intentions, goodwill, and good instincts were its obvious components. If, occasionally, a hint of extreme soberness, even somberness, broke through the easy façade, his friends, the other merchandise administrators and the buyers with whom he was most friendly, could understand it. Frustration over the staid corporate environment and over the seemingly slow advancement could do that to anyone. Working within a closed frame of tradition and conservatism could certainly add a damper. Advancement within any large company was never steady or ordered. It seemed to come in occasional, major gulps and then a wallowing for arid years at the same level in the organization.

In the meantime, he now had a growing family. In 1949, he had met Myra Schuss on a blind date at a Tanglewood, Massachusetts music festival, and they were married the next year. Their first son, Mitchell, was born in 1952 and they were to have two others, Daniel, in 1954 and Robert in 1958.

Down in the Macy coils—there were many merchandise administrators and their offices were on lower floors and only slightly less spartan than the lowly buyers'—Finkelstein could only be keenly aware and sensitive to the major personalities on the thirteenth floor. The big name and influence were, of course, both Jack Straus. But it was becoming increasingly obvious that "Mr. Jack" was more comfortable as the company's outside personification, its presence at city and community functions, much like big Bernard Gimbel, at his flagship store just a block away, the suave Nathan Ohrbach, the founder of the Ohrbach's fashion chain just up the block on Thirty-fourth Street, and tempestuous George Farkas, the founder of Alexander's Inc., the New York fashion chain then preparing to open its new flagship store on upper Lexington Avenue just opposite Bloomingdale's. But the intensifying competition with them, as well as with Sidney Solomon, the chairman of Abraham & Straus in Brooklyn and with the Bloomingdale's duo, Jim Schoff and Jed Davidson, had to be engineered by professionals who kept their noses to the grindstone and the cash register and didn't very often show them at public functions. Over the years, "Mr. Jack" would look dourly upon those of his top executives who were caught from time to time in the public spotlight. That was his role alone, not only because he was the chief executive but by family right and ownership. He didn't say it outright but everyone knew it.

That group of Macy's top pros, however, was a very mixed blend of talent, spark, and malaise. They were a group of men who had mostly come up the ranks much governed and influenced by the conservative leanings and social aspirations of "Mr. Jack." And in his own quiet, prim way, he made them all dance to his tune. Everyone could see it, the young, promotion-eager young executives no less than anyone.

Some of Finkelstein's contemporaries—and rivals in that ascendancy race—would often meet at lunch or during a break and talk about their heroes and villains in the upper ranks and how those men hovered successfully or vainly around the aristocratic figure of "Mr. Jack." There were Bob Lauter, who seemed to love the furniture business; Herbert Wexler and Elliott Jaffe, two merchandisers who built a solid reputation for their knowledge of the ready-to-wear business; and Robert Warner, who was also at home in the hard goods side of the business. There were others, too, who would join the group or make up a group of their own including Finkelstein. Sometimes, as they discussed the antics of the bosses, it was hard to decide whether to laugh, cry, feel awed or confused. For underneath the dignified, flannel-coated exterior of all those superiors were human beings with the frailties, mores, prejudices, and quirks that you would never expect in that most traditional, buttoned-up atmosphere of R. H. Macy. But there were others, too, who broke through the "Mr. Jack"–Macy matrix into distinguished careers in other companies and institutions.

There were, for example, James Schoff and Jed E. Davidson, who put excellent personal performances at Macy's behind them to bow to the wiles of Federated Department Stores, which wanted to transform the Bloomingdale's division into a greater money-maker. Though the Manhattan store was within strolling distance of many of New York's richest people, it had not really catered to them but consistently appealed to a lower-middle class, offering barrages of price cuts as the draw. Higher-priced goods sold at regular prices would automatically raise profits, but first the image of Bloomie's had to be drastically altered. Schoff and Davidson moved uptown as Bloomie's president and chairman, respectively, and in a matter of a few years, they transformed the group of promotional department stores into an innovative operation catering to the upper-middle class, the wealthy of New York, and well-heeled foreign tourists. In just a few years, they stunned retailing with their accomplishments. Their move preceded Finkelstein's entry into Macy's training squad by a few years, but that dramatic turnaround only served to inflame the imaginations of the young Macy executives.

And so did Walter Hoving, a tall, ascetic, domineering executive whose elitist demeanor masked both a deep ego and the taste of a fine artist. In a circuitous route, he left his Macy post as a top soft-line merchandiser to take key jobs at The Fair in Chicago, Lord & Taylor and Bonwit Teller in New York, and then Tiffany, where he eventually became principal owner. "He was acknowledged to be one of Macy's most esthetic merchants," said David Yunich. "For the younger men, it was a marvelous opportunity to learn from him and from Schoff and Davidson."

At Tiffany, Hoving developed his own exclusive designers such as Jean Schlumberger and Paloma Picasso, the talented daughter of the great painter. He also worked successfully to enhance Tiffany's image by inspiring his staff and suppliers to build up the silver and diamond business to new worldwide standards. What Schoff, Davidson, and Hoving did was not dissimilar. One can generalize that a striking new product or concept has the ability to create its own market. The novelty, presented first with dramatic but tasteful emphasis and then with variations, soon loses its stamp of novelty and becomes "innovation." That was basically their approach, varying according to their individual predilections. And that reality as it unfolded could hardly be overlooked by the itchy, youthful observers.

Howard Otten succeeded Walter Hoving as a major New York division merchandiser. He was a stern administrator but he would occasionally break out with a paternal smile at some of the well-intentioned foibles of the younger men under him.

When Ernestine Gilbreth, the adult game buyer in the New York division, announced that she was pregnant and would have to go on maternity leave, Otten decided to tap Dave Yunich, who was ready to be assigned to a buyer's post from the training squad. Macy had a very successful adult game department with variety and depth almost comparable to Abercrombie & Fitch, and the Herald Square store had an imposing room displaying a number of truly magnificent game tables. But Yunich was dismayed as he went around the game room to see that a good portion of the pool and other game tables were old stock. They had been there, he sensed, for some years, maintaining their sumptuous appearance but increasingly assuming the status of "overage inventory."

As the pro-tem buyer, the young Yunich didn't quite know what to do. But luck intervened. One day, the water sprinkler went off and he was summoned. Acting quickly, he moved all of the old game tables under the sprinkler, rightfully assuming that the department was covered by insurance. When the insurance adjuster studied the situation, he told Yunich, "That's quite a coincidence that all of these expensive game tables were right under the sprinkler."

Yunich scratched his head. "Gee, that was a coincidence, wasn't it?" he said. "I was just in the process of changing the game room around to rearrange our displays when it happened, you know, like an act of God." There was, of course, no way in which the adjuster could contest what the buyer claimed.

When Howard Otten heard about the incident, he told Yunich, "I think you get an A for ingenuity but a D for integrity." The curse, if there was any in his remark, was offset by a smile. It was a story that was told and retold around the store, becoming a minor Macy legend that was not lost on the open ears and minds of the Young Turks.

There were others, too, who left a mark. Beardsley Ruml, an economist who had also earned a doctorate in psychology and education at the University of Chicago, was appointed treasurer of R. H. Macy in 1934 and from 1945 through 1949 was its chairman of the board. He was also chairman of the Federal Reserve Bank of New York from 1941 to 1947, doubling in part as Macy's chairman. During wartime 1942, he proposed to the Senate Finance Committee a "Pay-As-You-Go" plan that would forgive all or part of the expected 1942 taxes so as to inaugurate a system of payroll deductions the following year. It immediately ran into resistance from both the Treasury Department and Congress, as well as from President Franklin D. Roosevelt, who regarded it as a plan that would favor wealthier taxpayers. But after an initial rejection of one version of the Ruml proposals, Congress adopted his basic program in 1943 and it became an official practice by July 1. The Ruml "Pay-As-You-Go" plan was later credited with an important role in helping the U.S. government finance the onerous costs of World War II. And later citizens, the bulk of whom surely forgot or didn't know Ruml, were able to benefit from paying their income tax on the installment plan.

At Macy, both as treasurer and chairman under Jack Straus, Ruml also developed what he called the "Macy Q sheet," containing the criteria by which department managers could have control of all the vital facts to effectively operate their departments. His efforts during the war and postwar years in the company convinced "Mr. Jack" of the strong priority of financial controls and later led to his appointment of another financial man, Don Smiley, as chairman and chief executive. Ruml liked to test his ideas first on younger men, knowing that their fresh approach was fertile ground for new seed. And he found that they liked being used as guinea pigs; it boosted their egos in a highly conventional, repressed environment.

As the decade of the forties ended, Straus briefly assumed the chairmanship of Macy but once again realized that he couldn't be both the company front man and the chief merchant. He then appointed a cousin, Robert Weil, the son of Jack's sister, Minnie Straus Weil, as company president. The apparent example of nepotism wasn't offensive to those who knew "Bobby" Weil, a bright, visionary executive with the courage of his convictions, even though his actions were sometimes controversial.

In 1952, Macy came to a watershed on one of its most important operating policies, its right to price goods any way it liked. While in Korvettes it found a ready competitor to match it and even prompt it to cut prices more, the other traditional department stores, such as Abraham & Straus, Gimbel Brothers, Bloomingdale's, and B. Altman mostly adhered to the prices set by major branded producers. Fair trade giving suppliers the right to specify the minimum retail price had functioned as a tight lock on retail pricing since the first statute was adopted in 1931 as a measure to stabilize the Depression economy. But the federal statute, supported by many state laws, had since come under severe pressure as discounters pushed against it. In 1952, in the latest court test of the law and the only successful one, Schwegmann Brothers, the New Orleans drugstore chain, won its case in a Louisiana State Court, giving sellers more latitude in setting their own prices. The startling effect of that reversal of the twenty-year-old law was to weaken the entire structure of fair trade and subsequent court cases were decided on the new precedent.

It was just before the 1952 Memorial Day weekend, when retail advertising normally booms. On Macy's thirteenth floor, a debate raged. Everyone knew it would now be open season to promote whatever prices one wanted. For years, Jack Straus had been Macy's strongest advocate of the "6 percent less for cash" policy that in effect allowed the chain to set its own prices, and as the guardian of the policy, Straus developed a keen sensitivity to those merchandisers and buyers who tried to fudge on that policy or to live up to it. But now, it seemed, all that was up in the air. With fair trade apparently moribund and with little likelihood that any price-setter would sue a price-cutter, it was clear that all of Macy's competitors would be freed of their binds and the "6 percent less" policy would be meaningless.

Straus wisely left the decision to his relative. Weil listened carefully to the arguments either for cutting the prices of all the brands that Macy's carried, thus inviting a donnybrook in the form of a heated price war, or else cutting prices selectively.

Finally, Weil declared emphatically, "We must protect our franchise with the public. We will cut the tags on every brand in the store." But the others warned him that such a move would open Macy's to widespread "pot-shooting" from all its competitors. None had all the variety and depth of merchandise that Macy did but all had several departments that could compete head-to-head with the same ones at Macy. The store's leading merchants told Weil that if Macy's cut prices across the board, Gimbel would take it on in the drug department with matching or deeper price reductions. Bloomingdale's would take on Macy's in its stationery and men's wear departments. Gertz of Long Island would take it on in books and so on. Weil, supported by Straus, was adamant.

Shortly after, Macy ran major advertising proclaiming that its "6 percent less for cash" policy allowed its customers to enjoy lower prices on many national brands. The expected happened. The other New York stores jumped in with selective price-slashing. Macy responded by slashing prices further, forced to take on all comers. Customers had a great time, shopping stores up and down Manhattan, in Brooklyn, and Long Island. Prices of many products became ridiculous, with the Monopoly game at one point selling in several stores for only 9 cents. The war went on for months, feeding on itself with the inevitable effect on store profits.

As 1952 ended, Macy's management was compelled to give its public shareholders some bad news. That year, the company suffered its first annual loss in its history. It taught the Macy people that they could no longer perform the role of "predatory price cutters," as more than a few suppliers labeled them. Instead, the company had to develop a rapport with the increasing number of branded producers in every field, adhering to a price pattern that wouldn't rile the suppliers but would eventually prompt them to offer more lines to Macy. And, for the first time, while Macy had offered installment credit for years but never charge accounts, its management decided to test those waters, too.

The lesson of that big price war was clear, leaving a ringing memory with the rising executives. If you're going to take on the whole world, at least do it on your own terms, with merchandise that the competition couldn't get, beg, steal, or buy. There was no point in giving the store away. Finding ways of attracting customers by exciting pricing that helped rather than hurt your profits was absolutely vital.

Rivalries among the rising young executives were expected and natural. Without years in which to fester, their expression was open and spontaneous, somewhat like boys elbowing or cuffing one another in a schoolyard. But in the more rarefied atmosphere of the thirteenth floor, the jousting among top executives was much more subtle, more inhibited, and deeper, lasting for years as rivals maneuvered their way up the narrowing pinnacle. And Ed Finkelstein, the young merchandise administrator, was the beneficiary of one of those lingering but no less bitter contests. It was a competition that rested not only on ambition but on conflicting personalities.

When Herbert Seegal was hired by Jack Straus as a senior merchant in the New York division, David Yunich was already president of the Bamberger's division. He had risen rapidly in big steps climaxed by being named senior vice-president for merchandising in New York. But when he was summoned by Weil and Straus and told that they were sending him to head the ailing New Jersey division as its president, Yunich was not wild about the idea. He did not want to be taken out of the flagship operation that in the 1950s was Macy's biggest divisional profit-maker to head Bam's, its poorest money earner.

Seegal, one of the few outside executives hired by Macy's for an important position, fitted in well in the New York division. But he was a new personality at Macy's, a quiet, introspective type. At multidivisional meetings, when the highest-level executives were gathered for a corporate review or brainstorming, it was obvious that he and the husky, extroverted Yunich sitting across the big table were two distinctly different types. Their rivalry, which was to grow bitter with the years, didn't actually surface for another eight years, when Seegal was appointed to succeed Yunich in New Jersey. It deepened even further as their separate careers advanced.

At Bam's, Yunich was at first dismayed by the vast, down-at-the-heels main store in Newark, sitting forlornly in a decaying area where urban blight had hurt retail business and discouraged shoppers. The big question, of course, was what to do with that huge store, acquired by Macy in 1929 from the Bamberger family. Annual volume at Bamberger in 1955, Yunich's first year at its helm, was only $82 million, but profits on sales were less than one-half of 1 percent. Macy's New York had sales of about three times that much with a profit of about 5 percent. Yunich set about his task, spending considerable time studying both competition and local and state demographics.

After about two years, he turned in a long-range plan, one covering the following three years, which showed that by the end of that period, Bam's would not have a larger volume than its New York counterpart but that its earnings would surpass it. The reaction in the company's headquarters was first amazement and then something like ridicule. Weil, who liked Yunich, nonetheless asked him, with some asperity, "What's this all about, Dave?"

"Well, since you sent me to Bam's, I've come up with a slogan."

"What is it?"

" 'I don't want to set the world on fire. I just want to burn up New Jersey.' "

Weil said nothing for a few moments. After he collected himself, he asked, "You think you can turn Bamberger's in three years from a division that does not even one-half of one percent profits to one that does six percent before taxes?"

"Yes."

"How, Dave?"

"I guess my slogan didn't catch on with you."

"Flesh it out for me."

"I'm convinced that the real future for Bam's isn't in the revival of the Newark store. I know that that is what you and Jack charged me with. But after some experience there now, there's no way that you can do that and have it mean anything. But there is a way to go that will have some real clout, and that is to capitalize on the great Bamberger name by taking it all over the state of New Jersey."

"And that," Weil asked, "is what you mean by, 'I just want to burn up New Jersey'?"

"Right, Bobby."

That, of course, was merely the first discussion of many before Yunich got the green light. It actually took him eight years to accomplish the feat, but by the time he did, Bamberger's had risen in annual sales to $500 million and its profits in both dollars and percentage of profit were the best in the corporation and among the highest in the nation. His reward was what he had wanted in the first place—to become president of Macy's New York—but when he was finally given that post, he wasn't so sure he wanted it. He had come to love Bamberger's and adjusted his life to it. But he couldn't fight the "supreme command from Jack." Straus told him, "We are going to use you over here. You've done your job there."

Yunich felt instinctively that much more could have been done at Bam's. He wanted to further implement his policy of giving the branch stores greater autonomy and diversity of stock and treating them as full-fledged stores rather than as outlying branches. He knew that the concept of separate buying executives and store operational executives needed more fleshing out. He was also convinced that Bam's could further develop top executives to provide more management depth.

But all that would have to be done by someone else. In the interim, Herb Seegal had made a considerable impression at the New York division. Seegal showed a fine sense for merchandising apparel and for developing competitive strategy, and despite his reserved manner, he could motivate younger men and women to not only perform better but throw themselves into their jobs with zeal. His drawback, colleagues said about him, was that sometimes he displayed more zeal than he had the ability to administer. Ironically, while Yunich wanted to be known as a skilled merchant, he was credited for being a fine administrator. And Seegal was seen more as a top merchant, whereas he craved to be known as an apt administrator. But Seegal made up for it by being not just a canny merchant but an adept speaker who knew how to apply the techniques of showmanship to inspire co-workers. On balance, he was a natural choice to succeed Yunich at Bam's and in 1962 he was named to that post.

Seegal now demonstrated a side of his nature that belied his low-keyed manner. In a short time, eagerly wanting to make his own imprint on Bam's beyond what Yunich had accomplished, he decided to reshuffle the top layers of the New Jersey executive ranks. During his decade at the New York division, he had had the opportunity to study the best talent there and to nurture it. And so he requested and got several of the most promising Macy New York executives to be

transferred to Bamberger's, in spite of opposition by the top management at Herald Square. Among the transfers was Ed Finkelstein, the
merchandise administrator, who was promoted several steps to be
Bamberger's senior vice-president and director of merchandising.

In the fourteen years at Macy's New York, Finkelstein had changed.
From an ambitious, young merchant with an occasional tentative
expression he had evolved into a hard-nosed, assured executive whose
ambition had soared along with his growing reputation. His ego, never
small, grew, too, under the lavish praise of Seegal and other superiors.
Finkelstein, friends noticed, was beginning to show signs of impatience by exploding at ill-defined or ill-conceived efforts by those
under him. Also observed was his evident conviction that personal
loyalty meant a great deal, even if it led to some sacrifices by the
individual. Unlike others who considered business relationships
friendships of convenience, he took them more seriously and held
close associates to obligations of goodwill, sometimes even when it
hurt. That was to become a core ingredient in his relationship with
others, especially later.

Finkelstein had learned much from all his predecessors, and particularly from the thirteenth-floor brass, whom he had carefully studied.
His knowledge as he advanced represented a synthesis of much of
their wisdom, but he was beginning to develop his own refinements.
Among them was the question of the relative worth of national brands
versus store labels, and he sensed that the 90 percent national brands,
10 percent store brands traditional ratio could justifiably be shifted
more toward the latter.

Another dawning question was whether the future of department
stores really lay in their being everything for everyone at a time when
some promising new specialty chains were sprouting. Should the
"everything" store, for example, continue to earn minimal profits or
none at all in departments that others were managing better by concentrating on them? Or would it be better to drop such merchandise as
sporting goods, pharmaceuticals, major appliances, or toys so as to bear
down on apparel, sportswear, housewares, jewelry, and cosmetics, on
which you could get higher markups? And if, perhaps, you could
combine the two burgeoning ideas—better national brands but more
store brands while concentrating on the departments with the best
return—who could tell what you could accomplish?

He had also developed a close team of devoted associates. When the summons came from Seegal to cross the Hudson, Finkelstein took a number of them along with him. They included Mark Handler, a buyer of women's sportswear; Philip Schlein, who bought women's apparel; and Herbert Friedman, first a buyer of women's dresses and then of drapery hardware. He later brought over Robert Friedman, who also bought women's apparel, and at Bam's Finkelstein found himself impressed by Arthur Reiner, a young buyer. If Finkelstein later recalled that there were some further protests from the New York group about the purloining of promising young talent from that division when he rationalized his 1986 leveraged buyout of the company as a means of retaining people who were being lured by others, he did not take notice of it.

Seegal and Finkelstein plunged into the situation at Bam's as if Yunich's turnaround efforts hadn't meant anything. "Ed quickly made his mark at Bam's," observes Herbert Mines, a New York executive recruiter who had been a Macy personnel vice-president. "Seegal and Finkelstein decided that Bam's was still an ordinary, staid, old-fashioned type of department store group. They decided to really make it over. And they imbued the team of people they had brought over from the New York division with considerable drive. It was a very cohesive bunch of guys."

Beginning early in his Macy career, Finkelstein welded his relationships with that group on both a social and professional basis. Most were tennis devotees and they often played together. They also lunched together and gathered their families together on weekends and some holidays. Finkelstein and Mark Handler built a warm rapport that was to last for decades. "Finkelstein those years at Bam's was a fortunate man," Mines resumed. "Herb Seegal ran interference for him and Handler took his rough edges off."

Others noted of those years that Seegal was widely respected, but his withholding personality did not lend itself to affection. Everyone, though, seemed to love Handler, a tall, handsome man whose smooth warmth was infectious and who always had time to listen to everyone's problems. Finkelstein came somewhere in between, very respected, generally liked except by those whom he offended by his push for greater results.

As they took what Yunich had done and improved upon it, Bam's slowly assumed the repute in the department store business as one of the sharpest, most efficiently run operations. The Seegal–Finkelstein–Handler team got more credit for their refinements and precedent-setting moves than Yunich did. But it was evident to those who track retailing for a long period that no new policies are that new and that they are usually based upon a bedrock of policies or breakthroughs that a predecessor has generated. Yunich built on what Felix Fuld did at Bam's; Seegal built on what Yunich had done; Finkelstein built on what Seegal did. And when Handler eventually succeeded Finkelstein at Bam's, he built on what his friend accomplished.

But whether Finkelstein could have gone so far so fast and then climbed even higher without Seegal, his mentor, is an open question. In business, as everyone sooner or later learns, one's advancement is often based on having a "rabbi" or "priest," someone in high places to push him forward, recommend him at the most strategic times and find ways of somehow elbowing him into the spotlight. That Finkelstein later broke with Seegal as the two got closer and closer to the pinnacle is a sad testimonial to the fact that when it involves two strong men with sizable egos, the relationship of mentor-student breaks apart.

But until Finkelstein became president and then chairman–chief executive at Macy's New York and he and Seegal began to battle, the older man was his loyal sponsor. Perhaps the most piquant irony in Finkelstein's entire career was that he was the happy beneficiary of Seegal's drive to show that he was a better man than Yunich. Without that basic rivalry between two ambitious executives, Finkelstein's career path and life—and Macy's progress, as well—might have been very different.

CHAPTER FOUR

BOOM AT BAMBERGER'S

As Bam's began to reverberate to the cool, disciplined drive of Herb Seegal, a natural curiosity centered on the new broom. He seemed so self-assured as he walked around the cavernous Newark store, with others in tow; he never allowed one hair to be ruffled on his sleek head, no frown to wrinkle his face as he confronted one after another of Yunich's actions or changes, studying each carefully as if he sought to ascertain its logic, its *raison d'être,* its soul. And then soon afterward the word would come down—do it differently.

It was this lack of emotion, deftly combined with aggressive decisions, that created the intrigue and curiosity about the new boss. He was quickly liked and respected, but his unusual combination of traits led some to wonder about him. Had he always been that combination of ice and fire, of an iron fist in a velvet glove?

Actually, he hadn't. Not long after Seegal had come from Richmond to New York, he had made an abrupt, 360-degree swing in personality and behavior.

After an unhappy marriage, Seegal had become a bachelor, pursuing a quiet life with few social demands in staid Richmond. But when he arrived in New York as the senior merchant for apparel, he soon found himself courted, wined and dined, by the major suppliers on Seventh Avenue. He became especially friendly with the Evans brothers,

Charles and Robert, who pursued an active role in jet-set society, New York night life, and Hollywood. The handsome Bob loved the movie capital and for some years he gravitated between assisting Charles in operating Evan-Picone, a well-known fashion house, in New York and producing or fostering movie productions on the coast. Later, Bob Evans resigned from Evan-Picone to become a successful producer of such movie blockbusters as *The Godfather.*

Seeing the lonely, ascetic life that Herb Seegal initially led in New York, Charles and Bob Evans invited him to dinners at New York's finest restaurants and to join them at the better nightclubs. Slow to accept at first, Herb eventually gave in and in due course became a frequent guest in Manhattan's best-known night spots. In the gossip columns in the *New York Daily News,* the *Daily Mirror,* and other newspapers, his name was often coupled with those of actresses and social swingers. Seegal didn't like that but, for the first time in years, he was enjoying himself socially.

But one day he was summoned by Jack Straus. Returning from the thirteenth floor, his face was red, his expression dour. When his closest associates asked him what was wrong, he said, "Well, I got the word. It's either show up in the gossip sheets or stay at Macy's." Seegal hesitated and added, "I said that I would stay at Macy's."

From then on, he resumed his solitary existence. "It was like he went into a cave," said a former associate. "He stayed home at night or worked late and never showed up anymore in the fleshpots. He became an entirely different person—reserved and remote."

It was classic "Mr. Jack" at work. No important Macy executive was to create notoriety, be caught in the spotlight of public attention, or otherwise disport himself in ways to give the wrong impression about the company. It was ironic that Herb Seegal, usually so proper and disciplined, would be the one to draw Straus's disfavor.

In time, Seegal recovered from the blow to his pride and proceeded to concentrate on making Bam's a better, more profitable business. Soon, he became a ubiquitous presence in the big store on Market Street. He wanted to know everything that was going on and, in fact, displayed a great command of these details. "For want of a nail, a kingdom was lost" became Seegal's credo.

But although he didn't trust others to take care of all the little things needed to ensure that the big things would work, he was primarily interested in the latter rather than the former. Operating on the two levels, he became a difficult man to work for, but the respect for him—

at first reluctant—grew, and as the division's profits mounted, it turned to awe.

As the Herald Square executives he had imported to Bam's watched him, they learned principles-cum-details that stayed with them and which helped build their own careers to unexpected heights. Finkelstein, in particular, benefited from Seegal's merchandising philosophy and the younger man used it to distinct advantage in subsequent stages of his Macy career. Shortly after joining Macy, Seegal expressed some dissatisfaction with the practice of "6 percent less for cash" and Macy's supporting advertising catchphrase, "The price is right." He declared, with a touch of sarcasm, "Sure the price is right but is the merchandise right?" He became infatuated with the principle that as competition grew, the stores that would stay on top would be those that took pains to stock precisely what customers wanted rather than what they thought customers wanted. It was an important distinction, but it was often ignored.

With Macy's extensive comparison-shopping department of one hundred women skilled at checking what shoppers wanted or didn't want at competitive stores as well as at Macy's, it wasn't hard to learn. This knowledge was buttressed by Seegal's willingness to listen to customers and to what others said customers wanted. He made his own observations, too. A bachelor with time to spare, he shopped every manner of stores. It was the merchant's curse. Details, details—everyone seemed to ignore them. Sometimes, it appeared, the boss was the best "detail" man.

Turning to his coterie of "personal interns," Seegal would say, "Look, let's take men's oxford cotton shirts. If there are guys who like them in white, tan, blue, yellow, let's have them all. And let's have them in sizes from shrimp to giant, if that's what we need. And let's have them in the big national and designer brands and in our own brands. We've got to be in the business of having every size, color, and version that people want in every damn category they want."

"But, Herb, won't that excessively build up our inventories?" one in the group would ask.

Herb gave him that cool, searching appraisal that frequently made an underling's heart pound. "Sure it will," he said. "But if we make sure we know what the customer wants and stock it, that inventory will disappear pretty quickly."

More than a decade later, when he was president of the Macy's New York division, Finkelstein was asked if he felt that the fourteen stores would have enough merchandise for the forthcoming Christmas season. The question was based on the growing customer complaints that too many stores were operating with thin stocks, apparently running scared in a difficult economy. "We're in good shape," replied Finkelstein. "Take a look. We've got it all. Our policy is that we build our inventory so that if there's an unanticipated sales bulge of 10 percent, we can easily handle it."

"So won't that give you high markdowns?"

"Maybe. But if you know your business, you can even make money on markdowns."

Finkelstein was nominally the head of the group of hot M.B.A.'s from the New York division, and his enthusiasm and ability to articulate to the others what was important and needed endeared him to Seegal. Seegal saw in the determined, serious young man more than a hint of great future responsibility. Finkelstein not only had the brains, he had the enthusiasm and the hard drive that Seegal knew were so needed in the head-crushing retail business. Once Seegal said to him, "For years, Macy's has been pushing 'the price is right.' But Marvin Traub's been getting all the upscale business at Bloomie's. That's not smart." Finkelstein nodded and stored away that admonition.

Walter F. Loeb, who later shifted from retailing to become one of the most respected of securities analysts on Wall Street, worked as a buyer under Herb Seegal at Bam's. "What began to happen as Seegal and Finkelstein looked into every corner of Bamberger's and promoted new programs was that a lot of the excitement that had been associated with Macy's Herald Square shifted to Newark," Loeb said. "It wasn't only merchandising and presentation. It was the store events, too, like flower shows, international import fairs, and celebrity luncheons. Bam's came alive."

Personally hired by Seegal after Loeb had worked several years in the advertising department of Macy's New York, the new Bam's buyer was assigned to the Newark store's basement lingerie department. "I knew lots of people 'upstairs' were feeling the pressure from the new broom," he said, "but we never did in the basement. We had our own pressures of constantly promoting price to bring the customers downstairs. So, that aside, I never felt that I was being pushed too hard. What we were all conscious of was that Bamberger's was turning into a real, exciting store and that in turn made everyone working there excited."

But Loeb found himself unhappy in a basement position. His progress at Macy had proved slow. It took him seven years to become a buyer, partly because he had not entered in the executive training squad.

After nine years, Loeb left the Macy organization for an "upstairs" post as lingerie buyer at Gertz Long Island. A few years later, in 1974, he returned to Macy in its Queens, New York, store as a merchandise manager. By that time, Seegal had been promoted from Bam's chairmanship to the corporate presidency of R. H. Macy. "He came into the Queens store one day not long after I rejoined the company," Loeb recalled, "and he was unusually warm to me. It was like a welcome back. I often wondered how he remembered me from down in Bam's basement. But I guess that's the way he was, nothing escaped him. But it—and seeing some of the old faces—made me feel that I was being brought back into the family."

Like Loeb, the executive "interns"—Ed Finkelstein, Mark Handler, Herb Friedman, Bobby Friedman, and Phil Schlein—were ever-conscious of advancement. If the details, the countless impedimenta of the department store business, sometimes imposed a burden on the mind and memory, they realized that Seegal's pressure on them was only a way of getting a handle on the business and was also the way to get ahead. All became apt students of the business, working long hours, poking their heads into all corners of the store and its seven branches. Advancement had a set equation. Closeness to the decision-maker plus the proper rung on the pecking order plus enthusiasm and talent equaled the next step up. The equation repeated, favored by some luck, should inevitably lead to the presidency of a full store division.

But, of course, first a vacancy had to open. The result was a game of musical chairs, put in play by the decision-maker. For example, when Yunich moved up from president of Bam's to president of New York, Seegal became president of Bam's. In order to get Finkelstein over to Bam's, two weeks after his own appointment, Seegal arranged the transfer of A. Alfred Landisi, senior vice-president and director of merchandising for ready-to-wear at Bam's, to a similar post at the New York division in exchange for Finkelstein. The others were brought over soon after, and as Bam's fortunes shone, each was advanced. In 1965, Herb Friedman was promoted to Bam's vice-president for budget store (basement operations) from merchandise administrator. The same year, Mark Handler was promoted from vice-president to senior

vice-president and director of merchandising. In 1966, Phil Schlein
was advanced to vice-president from merchandise administrator. The
youngest of the group, Bobby Friedman, who had joined Bam's while
attending Rutgers University in 1962, the year Seegal came to Bam's,
became a vice-president in 1968. But the one who enjoyed the fastest
advancement was Ed Finkelstein, who within months of coming to
Bam's in 1962 was moved up from senior vice-president to executive
vice-president for merchandising and sales promotion.

As his titles became more imposing, Finkelstein displayed a harder
patina. Those who would sit with him at weekly executive committee
meetings began to see a greater self-confidence, a tendency toward
abrasiveness that some found disturbing. He showed impatience when
an underling seemed unable to understand the cold logic and irrefuta-
ble facts that he presented. Over the years from 1962 through 1969,
Finkelstein became a subtly and not so subtly different person. The
smiling diffidence of a promising young executive in his twenties and
thirties in New York gradually shifted to the demanding personality of a
second-in-command in his forties in Newark.

"When I first met him at Bam's, I thought I had him sized up as a
smart, upwardly mobile guy," observed an executive who faced him for
years at such meetings. "But as I worked with him and saw him in
action, it seemed to me that he was becoming more complex.
Undoubtedly, he was very bright. And he was a solid merchant who
felt that there was no substitute for the fundamentals of the business.
But I also saw him becoming combative, ruthless, and arrogant. He
was never ambivalent about anything. But he was also very careful not
to brush up against Herb Seegal, his mentor."

In a sense, said this executive and others, Finkelstein had the best of
both worlds. He was the center of a smoothly functioning mechanism
that wrought great changes in its own world, that of the growing
Bamberger's chain. And he was the eager disciple of a great merchant,
Seegal, who willingly imparted his knowledge and skills. The protégé,
in turn, imparted what he learned from Seegal, as well as his own
refinements, to a harmonious circle of executives—Handler, the two
Friedmans, Reiner, Schlein, and others. He could easily ignite their
enthusiasm and their personal drives; they were right for each other.
Finkelstein carried out Seegal's commands and insulated him from
opposition or controversy. His own loyal crew carried out his demands
and insulated him from the turmoil that change created. All of it
worked as long as the results satisfied the thirteenth floor at Herald

Square. And they did. Bam's sales and earnings grew dramatically every year, not just because of the new stores that were opened but at "comp" stores, those matured units where volume can erode unless they are carefully monitored. Gains there were more important than total results and were the true measure of performance in the retail business.

Shifting the division's stance to more customer-oriented merchandise, it was inevitable that there would be resentment, even an outcry in the supplying markets.

For decades, buying merchandise from producers and importers was often consummated at management-to-management lunches, cocktails, and dinners. Thus, a social relationship created a proper environment in which departmental buyers later could meet the manufacturer's salesmen and write the actual order. But in his zeal to stock "customer-demand" goods, Seegal frowned on that type of contact. In fact, he instructed Bam's merchandise and buying staff that the new Bam's wouldn't buy just anything that was available. Based on its improved knowledge of what the shoppers wanted, Bam's would select what it deemed most likely to sell. And it would go one step further. Presented with such goods, it would sample only a small order. Bam's buyers were told to buy only one style in any new group of goods. "The public will decide if it likes V-neck sports shirts or crew-neck sports shirts," Seegal said. "Or long hemlines or short hemlines. And we'll know in a day or two."

Suppliers were horrified by this example of merchandising heresy. How could they live with a retail account that not only cherry-picked but cherry-picked from that? Obviously, they couldn't plan their production with such a buying approach. If the retailer didn't know whether the public would like V necks or crew necks or long or short hemlines, how would the producer know how much fabric to buy, how to schedule his production, and how many people to hire for the total effort? The risk, it became painfully clear, would fall upon the supplier's neck.

Finkelstein took a lot of the nasty telephone calls that resulted. But, as the system began to pay off for Bam's, their insistence took less effort as the suppliers realized that the new Bam's was doing what was right for it, although not necessarily for anyone else.

As he stalked the Bam's store seeking to present the new merchandise in its most appealing, productive manner, Finkelstein asked his display and internal design people to devise new ways of showing it in the store. Those specialists, though surprised by the sudden attention to their work, found themselves excited by the challenge to dramatize the settings in which merchandise was being sold. There were unused corners, forgotten outposts that could be put to use. And there were ways of showing clothes, appliances, furniture—every manner of product, no matter how utilitarian—in settings that would naturally enhance their practical and aesthetic values. The objective, of course, was to make the shopper see the goods as though she had never seen them before.

There was one showcase experience. Seegal and Finkelstein had inherited a large but unproductive branch store in Cherry Hill, New Jersey, whose proximity to Philadelphia, just across the Delaware River, and large size amid other not very competitive stores on the Jersey side seemed to offer more potential than the store had realized. As the team huddled over the goal of improving each branch store so that it could be more self-sustaining, Seegal challenged everyone to use the Cherry Hill store as a laboratory. It would be used to test major stock depth, the new, more interesting presentation, and greater inventory turnover. For months, the group applied itself to the task of transforming a dowdy, unimpressive 200,000-square-foot store into a money-making enterprise. "It was a great learning process for all of us," Phil Schlein recalled. "It gave us the ability of operating a true, multistore business while also producing a revitalized branch store."

As the 1960s approached a new decade, Bam's top team found its efforts being recognized and rewarded. The Newark-based division was making the whole company sit up and take notice. Executives of other companies wanted to come and see what was going on.

For Finkelstein, there was a sense of growing fulfillment. He had learned many new techniques, tested himself with ideas of merchandising, display, and presentation that he had never known in New York. And he had honed a practice of gentle and then not-so-gentle handling of people beyond anything he had known before. R. H. Macy appeared to recognize it, raising his remuneration and his bonuses. He had every reason to surmise that he would someday move up to head Bam's as its president when Seegal advanced up the ladder.

But Finkelstein never was to be given that post. One day in 1969, he was summoned to Herald Square and was told that he was needed in California. Things weren't going well there. Instead of at Bam's, where he had learned and achieved so much, he would reach his ambition of divisional president on the West Coast, based in San Francisco.

CHAPTER FIVE

CROSSFIRE
AT UNION SQUARE

They faced one another like so many scarred battlewagons, huge but depleted, wheezing from years of difficult but fruitless effort. Their future as stores was vague, doubtful, not promising.

San Francisco's urban park, Union Square, was still the carriage-trade center, but only a block or so to the west prostitution, drugs, and crime flourished. That was the disturbing paradox of Union Square, unaccountably still the city's great fashion center, though well past its prime.

Macy's California, I. Magnin, City of Paris (later to be known as Liberty House), and a group of smaller stores confronted each other on or near the square. Emporium Capwell stood two blocks away with its cavernous, gray hulk. Nearby were Bonwit Teller, Joseph Magnin, Gump's, Brooks Brothers, Cartier, and others.

The heady competition of the 1960s had been set in motion in the 1940s. In 1945, Macy's had acquired the old O'Connor Moffat and Company store, changed its name and made it the company's California flagship. I. Magnin, a lush store with imposing crystal chandeliers and gold-bronze display cases, arrived on the square in 1948. City of Paris, opened in 1910, had garnered a fine reputation for its couture fashions and extensive wine cellar, but, in 1972, it was purchased by Amfac Incorporated, a Honolulu-based conglomerate that also owned

59

the Liberty House department stores in California and Hawaii. Under Amfac, City of Paris became Liberty House, but the old store was soon closed and sold to Carter Hawley Hale Stores, a Los Angeles–based retail chain. That company, deciding that Liberty House retained some solid, local identity, opened a new store under that name just a few blocks from the square at Stockton and O'Farrell streets.

For a long time, however, another department store, not Macy's or I. Magnin or Liberty House, had owned the Bay customers. The Emporium, owned by Carter Hawley Hale Stores and later combined with that concern's Capwell stores, was one of the West Coast's most venerable establishments. Introduced to San Franciscans in 1896 by the Davis family, which had operated the Golden Rule Bazaar that had flourished during the California Gold Rush, the Emporium building was jerry-built and suffered severe damage in the great 1906 earthquake that leveled much of San Francisco. In 1908, the Davises rallied by building a new Emporium, featuring a great, central dome and the then most modern fixtures. Decades later, while that store on Market Street suffered through considerable area erosion, it remained an imposing edifice, a testament to the era when stores were designed with cathedral-like dimensions and ceilings.

The others, from Saks Fifth Avenue to Brooks Brothers, were of much more recent vintage, as the corporate owners of each specialty store chain leapfrogged across the country. The lure, of course, was northern California's gold coast and the state's rapidly growing financial, insurance, entertainment, and aerospace industries.

But by the end of the 1960s, the center of the California retail industry had slowly shifted to the proliferating, flowing suburbs of the Bay Area. Like the core areas of many other American cities, downtown San Francisco, especially Union Square, seemed to have lost much of its momentum and *raison d'être*.

On an afternoon in 1969, a middle-aged, chunky, New Rochelle native stood outside Macy's store and gazed at Union Square. As he told some of his new colleagues at the store, Ed Finkelstein felt a strong sense of displacement. At forty-four, he had spent fourteen years in the New York stores, six in the New Jersey division, and here he was plunked down in California. He was eager to tackle the new assignment, working with Jim Lundy, the previous division chief, but, he admitted, his heart was still back at Bam's and New York.

Nonetheless, he meant business, as everyone would soon find out.

People would resent it, even the good pros that were already there who thought that they were doing things right. Maybe they were, individually, but as a ship's complement, to borrow an old Navy term, they weren't sharp.

He had brought out his family with some trepidation. Myra, his wife, had her own activities and hobbies and would require some adjustment. And the boys had their problems. Mitchell, the oldest, who was aggressive, highly active, would miss his friends. Daniel, the middle one, a different type, soft-spoken, rather retiring, and Robert, the youngest, had medical problems. Moving the family, integrating them into a new environment for an indefinite, perhaps permanent, period, would also take some doing.

Finkelstein knew one thing, he told his closest friends back East. He would have to take care of his family at all times, though he did not want to be irrational, or unreasonable about it. He planned to bring the two older boys, Mitchell and Dan, into the business. He hoped that they would be interested, but even if not . . .

Touring the store, listening to the others at executive committee meetings, shopping the competition, what to do soon fell into place. The things that were done at Bamberger's would certainly work with the California division. But, as he soon discovered, there was a more leisurely lifestyle that would need some interesting tickling in merchandise. Blessed by some of the best weather in the world, Californians were more prone to live outdoors, to dress in a more unrestrained manner, and to adorn their homes with a zestiness blending western and Spanish styling. Californians, in fact, seemed to relish the rather envious complaints from easterners that their grooming and homes were not complementary and even clashed. This individuality in taste and feisty self-confidence had already created a California style that had filtered across the nation, indeed abroad. Hadn't the jeans craze, the beach bum prototype, and the lavish barbecue parties originated there? If not, they were certainly identified as West Coast creations.

"Ed began to reposition the twelve Macy stores in the Bay Area from very moderate-priced, promotional stores into a fashion-aware business aimed at the middle- and upper-income customer," said Philip Schlein. "He took on Bullock's North, Federated's local division. It was the fashion business in the area, but when Macy traded up and everyone in the stores pitched in, it was all over for Bullock's North. A few years later, Federated packed in that division."

Gradually, Finkelstein tackled each department, concentrating on the big-ticket merchandise in the home furnishings department, especially furniture and floor coverings, because the profits could be more substantial than in soft lines. Promoting likely candidates to higher posts and bringing in talented outsiders, he began changing the players in the stores, eagerly ferreting out younger people anxious to advance. Once the new pattern took shape, the role of Jim Lundy, the top management holdover with whom Finkelstein co-directed the California stores, waned considerably. Jack Straus and Don Smiley, who were running the corporation when it decided to make the management shift in California, weren't quite sure what to do with Lundy, but when they saw what Finkelstein was attempting to do and the early reaction to it, Lundy decided to resign within a year of Finkelstein's arrival.

Much has been written and discussed about "The Cellar," the basement chain of "shops" that replaced the traditional, shoddy budget levels of the Macy stores around the country. The attractive complex of departments selling housewares, gourmet food, and candy, with a barroom type of restaurant and contemporary fashion shops, caught on quickly; it seemed to capture the changing mood of the Bay Area. The first "Cellar" was introduced in the flagship San Francisco store in 1973, the next to last year Finkelstein remained in California and was soon replicated in other Macy units in the area. Eventually, "Cellars" sprouted in each of the major Macy stores. The lifestyle and women's pages of hundreds of newspapers and magazines hailed the "Cellar" as the epitome of late-twentieth-century merchandising, and countless competitive department stores set up their own versions. That reincarnation of the fading basement store, as part of and along with "the store as theater," became an important new symbol in Finkelstein's professional escutcheon.

But did Finkelstein create "The Cellar"? Some believed that he had copied the concept from Harrods in London. Executives who were there and some who followed say that it was really spawned by a group of executives. Probably the truth is that the concept of a basement arcade of shops marrying the tastes of a leisurely life and the ego-satisfying demand for fashionable goods for the person and the home was the result of Finkelstein's urging of the staff to originate a vehicle to satisfy those yearnings. "In those days, Ed would talk to his people, take feedback and listen to you," one Macy executive said.

Another executive who had worked for Finkelstein in California described him then as "a wonderful, warm, compassionate man. You could talk to him on a personal basis. One day, after I had demonstrated a pretty good performance for a couple of years, I said to him, 'Ed, will I ever make any money in this business?' 'How old are you?' Ed asked me. I told him and he said, 'You will. You're young enough and you'll do well. I like the way you have been operating.' Ed then took me to lunch and he was very gracious. He said that he wanted to get to know me."

Having his own crew of loyal subordinates with whom he felt socially at ease was an old Finkelstein need. "They made it like a club, at breakfasts, lunches, and dinners," said Larry Shapiro, who in the 1970s was a top apparel merchandiser at Macy's California, and had worked with Finkelstein in New York in the 1960s. "I was moderately friendly with Finkelstein, but I didn't want to spend the time required to make it more because I wanted to have a proper relationship with my family," Shapiro said. "All of them, especially Ed, wanted to have a personal relationship.

"Ed would say to me, 'I want to have the people around me that I enjoy. I spend so much time at work that I might as well enjoy it,'" Shapiro recalled. "But the strange thing was that he was so obsessed with his family, too. Yet he still wanted to have that club of his at work."

The fact was that in San Francisco, even several years after arriving there, the New Yorker missed his close colleagues and friends back at Bam's and New York. Far away, he sensed that his appointment had plunged him into a difficult, tense situation. Besides Lundy, with whom it was obvious that he would be grappling in "a battle for the throne," as a close colleague described it, there were others near the top who would fight him because he was the new boss. They had been there for some time and believed that they knew the local market and its peculiar quirks far better than he. Even after Lundy departed for a post at Mervyn's, the promotional apparel retail chain operated in the area by Dayton Hudson Corporation, Finkelstein knew that his isolation and the opposition would continue unless he built his own team. As he developed it, he also sought to find young men whom he could nurture and train and whom he could also make personal friends. He had done it back East and he meant to do it in the West. The difference was that he hadn't grown up with any of them on the West Coast as he had back East. "He was very adept at seeing the depth of young people," said the executive who had found him "warm and compassionate." "He found them often before anyone else did. But what he demanded was intense, personal loyalty."

* * *

Whether Finkelstein felt a need for urgency or not—his tenure in California was only to last five years—he pushed for rapid results. His experience at Bam's had taught him that no matter how well an urban flagship store could be restrategized and turned into theater, the flow of demographics and changing consumer mores was more in the direction of the suburbs, where the big regional malls were reaping more and more of the area's retail business. The flagship had to be the store group's paragon, in look, taste, and merchandise. Suburban customers might not come into the city to brave the traffic, parking, and crime problems, but Macy's ads and windows downtown could only build confidence or the lack of it in terms of the customer's own local store. The lesson of the decaying Newark store had been well learned and so had the principle of developing a multistore program under which every branch store was just as important and needed as much attention as the older store downtown.

Accordingly, he and his burgeoning team spent much time in the dozen branches, adapting and refining many things that had been instituted at Union Square. And both business and profits began to reflect the changes. Finkelstein had his eye on achieving a total group volume of $1 billion and a net income of $100 million, and he spurred his people on to that goal. One store, in Richmond, California, seemed incapable of resuscitation and he closed it, but in 1973, he more than replaced its volume with a new store in the East Ridge Mall in San Jose. It embodied everything that he had tried to do on Union Square, which had reflected what he had done in New Jersey. The early response was promising.

And as Finkelstein dug in and Macy's rivals responded, it became gradually clear that a fight for survival was under way. The pressure wasn't just on the Bullock's North group, supposedly the fashion leaders, but also on the two Magnins—I. and Joseph Magnin, which were not related—and, even more directly, on the Emporium, the volume leader in the area. In the case of the two Magnins, the swath cut two ways. I. Magnin, which catered to the wealthy and more affluent customers, found that Macy's was trading up and eating into its clientele, so I. Magnin's management began trading down a bit to meet Macy's head on. But, swimming in a different kind of pool, I. Magnin wasn't comfortable and did not perform smoothly, not meshing its new mixture of prices in a manner to encourage its customers. Joseph Magnin, owned by Amfac Inc., the Hawaiian pineapple and retailing conglomerate, discovered that its customers seemed inclined to upgrade their purchases at Macy's, just one city block away. Though Joseph Magnin opted to trade up to cope with the revitalized Macy, its customers wouldn't buy it. With more than twenty stores spread throughout the Bay Area, Joseph Magnin had established itself as a low- to middle-price purveyor and its halting efforts to change its public image failed. A few years after this abortive program, Joseph Magnin joined the demise of Bullock's North, persisting with going-out-of-business sales that lasted for months.

The big impact, however, was on the Emporium. The imposing flagship, with its great dome, grand stairway, and glass roof garden, and its ten suburban branches, felt Macy's push as it might a punishing storm. The Emporium, one of the two Carter Hawley Hale Stores, along with the Capwell stores in adjacent Oakland, had the benefit of a broad-based-income clientele, but its core was middle-income customers, many of whom were young marrieds and upwardly mobile singles and families. Management, aided by Carter Hawley's chief executive, Philip M. Hawley in Los Angeles, sought to broaden the Emporium's appeal by remodeling, enriching the merchandise, and adopting more creative sales promotion methods. The war quickened, somewhat like the classic battle in New York between Macy's and Gimbels, with each San Francisco group gaining through the frontal swipes against their other competitors.

The main survivors—Macy, the Emporium, and I. Magnin—undoubtedly were sustained because of the unwavering support of their well-heeled parents, R. H. Macy, Carter Hawley Hale, and Federated Department Stores, respectively. But the latter felt the cost and effort of supporting the five Bullock's North stores weren't as productive as developing its strong Bullock's South stores in the Los Angeles area. Joseph Magnin lost its backing from Amfac, which was involved in activities other than retailing.

In shoring up the Emporium, Phil Hawley made a daring move. He lured David Folkman, a much-respected, senior apparel merchant at Macy's California, to move over to the competition as the president of the Emporium. The youthful Folkman, a level-headed, low-key type, pitched in with zest at the Emporium, adapting some of the new Macy's methods and earning little of Finkelstein's ardor. Anyone who left Macy's, especially to go to the competition, was a "traitor," violating the trust that Macy had placed in him.

Toward the end of his California tenure, Finkelstein showed an increasing testiness and impatience toward any internal opposition or questioning about his moves. When he brought his older son, Mitchell, into the division as a junior executive, it did not sit well with some of the senior divisional officers. Finkelstein asked Orris Willard, the senior vice-president for construction and store planning, to talk to his son and give him the benefit of his counsel. But Willard, a frank, hard-hitting type who didn't swerve from offending others if he thought it necessary, behaved in character, according to others who were there at the time. Eyeing Mitchell's long hair, jeans, and generally unprepossessing appearance, Willard said, "If you're going to work here, young fellow, you're going to have to cut your hair and get cleaned up." At the next executive committee hearing, Finkelstein stared angrily at Willard and lashed into him for his handling of Mitchell.

In November 1974, Smiley and Seegal in New York phoned Finkelstein to tell him that they were bringing him back to the main division to help turn it around. His successor, they said, would be Phil Schlein, the Philadelphia-born, senior vice-president for merchandising at Bamberger's. Schlein had graduated from the University of Pennsylvania, majoring in engineering and architecture. But before he left Penn, he decided to switch to liberal arts and then sought to find a promising job in business. He joined Macy's executive training squad in 1957, the year he graduated from Penn, and soon advanced up the ladder as an assistant buyer, group manager, petite apparel buyer, and, eventually under Finkelstein, the merchandise administrator. He was one of the Young Turks brought over to Bam's by both Seegal and Finkelstein.

"When Mark Handler told me in late 1973 that both Smiley and Seegal wanted to see me in New York," related Schlein, "I had a real inkling that I was moving up. And when they told me that I was moving out to California to succeed Finkelstein, I was pleased. It was a very exciting challenge. But I had some mixed feelings. I had a thirteen-year-old girl and a nine-year-old son from a previous marriage and it would mean that I would have to leave them back East. But I couldn't refuse such a promotion at Macy's."

When he flew to California in December 1973, Schlein found Finkelstein jovial and friendly. "We had been close and I had kept in touch with him," Schlein said. "There was no reason to think that anything would go wrong. I knew that he had created a strong, new foundation out there and that I could take over because we held the same convictions." Finkelstein introduced him to every senior and many junior executives in the Union Square store. He made it a point also to introduce Phil to community leaders, so that the transition would be smooth. And Finkelstein and Myra gave several dinner parties for Schlein to meet others at their English Tudor home in suburban Hillsborough.

The Finkelsteins flew East and Schlein took over what his predecessor had wrought. The shoot-out at Union Square had quieted, the easterner had done well in the West, and everything appeared serene. In January 1974, "when I took over," Schlein said, "I thought that the California division was at least pointed in the right direction. Its mixture of merchandise was uneven and we didn't have a fine ready-to-wear or men's clothing operation. We needed further strength in achieving our goals. We needed more strong people and a lot of stores needed remodeling. But a good foundation had been laid by Ed. I was happy and excited to take over."

That situation, however, was due to change drastically in a few years as was the harmonious relationship between the two men. And it wasn't just the distance between both coasts that was responsible. The temperament of each was changing and ambition, never far from the surface, would eventually turn friends into enemies.

CHAPTER SIX

"I'M SICK AND TIRED OF HEARING ABOUT BLOOMIE'S!"

For days on end, Finkelstein stalked the store. Perhaps he felt that by searching into all its aisles, corners, outposts, reserve stockrooms, and dusty crannies, he could find what secrets the immense plant was withholding from its management. Somewhere there must be hints, some signals in those outposts; big stores have hundreds of them. Yet he found nothing, he told his colleagues, other than that much of the Herald Square store seemed unproductive, wasted, supporting those holdovers from the former management who insisted that the store's selling space had to be cut down.

He and his new team—again he freely purloined others from the sister divisions—also toured the rival stores: Bloomie's, of course; Saks Fifth Avenue; Bergdorf's; Bonwit's; Gimbels; Abraham & Straus; B. Altman; Bendel. They also took to the highways to cover the 170 miles encompassed by his division's sixteen stores, ranging from Manhattan through Long Island, Westchester County, Rockland County, and Connecticut—as far as Albany. They should have been a powerful group, a skein of stores tapping most of the major areas in the greater New York metropolitan area. But their energy seemed to be sapped, flagging morale and bad service symptomatic of their illness.

In New York City, Macy's huge size and presence throughout the city also should have delivered solid results but didn't. Besides the two-million-square-foot Herald Square flagship, there were branches in Brooklyn on congested Flatbush Avenue and in the successful Kings Plaza Shopping Center. There was also the "store-in-the-round" in the Elmhurst section of Queens, a Colosseum-like establishment that Dave Yunich had fostered in a flair of architectural daring. Collectively, the group was New York's biggest cluster, but you wouldn't know it from its meager profits.

Suppliers, competitors, customers, and stockholders eagerly told Finkelstein that Macy's New York had surrendered its clout to stores like Bloomie's, trading its quality reputation for a constant barrage of price-cutting promotions and special events. Sales would have been fair enough if they had been combined with an aggressive stance on fashion, well-known brand names, and strong visual impact, but it seemed to the new crew that the sixteen stores had given up their leadership. The result was routine. And as for the constant diet of price-cutting, it certainly did not spawn loyal customers; all it did was inspire them to seek bargains at Macy's or elsewhere, like fish darting at every bait. It was, Finkelstein told them flatly, no way to run a retail business.

Instead, he wondered, what if Macy's reorganized itself into a sort of "family retailer," with accent on upwardly mobile or upwardly affluent tendencies? But, someone rebutted, wasn't that exactly what Bloomingdale's was? He frowned and shrugged. So? Look what he and they had already done in both New Jersey and California. Macy's had attributes that Bloomie's didn't have. It sat on probably the most dense public transit hub in the world, Thirty-fourth Street and Broadway. It had a strong community hold with its highly awaited Fourth of July fireworks presentation and its Thanksgiving Day parade. But what Macy needed was a dimension of excitement, of theater, that would make shoppers' pulses race, that would wrest them out of their houses and apartments and bring them to Herald Square with wallets yearning to unload themselves.

He had no program, but he knew that he had to adapt what he had done in the other divisions to New York, that he had to alter the idea that the Herald Square store was the only important facility and give the branches new muscle and identity. The concept had worked so well at Bamberger's and was beginning to in San Francisco. Perhaps the way to start was to take the mammoth New York branch in the Roosevelt Field Shopping Center, in Garden City, Long Island, as a prototype of the new Macy's and test the validity of the combination of family appeal and dramatic presentation. That way, they could take the bugs out of a remodeling process before tackling the more expensive, more onerous task of redoing Herald Square.

The more he pondered the approach, the more grateful he was to that lowly sales manager at a Bamberger's branch who years ago had on his own initiative dressed up his background decor and general presentation of merchandise and thereby racked up impressive volume gains. If there were to be geniuses at the top, there had to be some geniuses at the bottom, too. It would do well to watch for them.

But the improvement of how you showed merchandise had to be only one element in the entire package. By the mid-1970s, everyone knew that you couldn't just sell the sizzle without the steak, the style without the substance. Others had tried it and flopped. What should Macy's New York sell; what departments should it concentrate on; what type, price, and brands of goods should it push that would give it not only better profits but, just as important, market leadership? People had to begin thinking of Macy's first, not second, third, and certainly not last.

And so Finkelstein made it a routine to talk to as many people as he could—customers, friends, suppliers—about their perception of Macy's. During 1974, he later estimated that he took to lunch almost two hundred of his executives, from seniors to juniors, picking their brains and throwing concepts at them. One of his professors at Harvard had emphasized the need to sound out co-workers and customers so that one's instincts are freed and broadened, and to tap the button of natural entrepreneurship that resides in many young executives. He went a step further, resorting to Peter Drucker's philosophy of autonomy, what the management guru termed "federalized decentralization," the policy of decentralized authority and centralized control. But, Drucker warned, that in itself could not be enough. "The challenge is going increasingly to be entrepreneurship and innovation," he insisted in his 1973 book, *Management.* He added, "What we need is the innovative organization—in addition to the managerial one."

In 1974, not long after he had returned to New York, Finkelstein wrote a memorandum to his executives spelling out his management approach in his new post.

Executives were put on notice that they were free to run their own shows, but they would be held accountable for the results. It was pure Drucker—establish high standards of character and integrity, maintain an open consultation with your executives and let the string of authority be loose enough so that they could show initiative. But periodically tighten the reins so that executives would know they would have to impose self-discipline because there was a reckoning on entrepreneurship. In a way, Finkelstein realized, it was tantamount to being a teacher, a role he liked, with alternate periods of instruction and examination.

Again, one of his brash, young executives observed, "It's kind of like Bloomie's, isn't it, Ed, giving the merchants their head? Isn't that what made them so successful?" Finkelstein grimaced, not answering.

Having decided that each store should be a full, independent entity of its own, that visual merchandising was the way to go and that only certain departments should receive the full treatment, Finkelstein voluntarily gave up some $35 million in annual sales by dropping a variety of low-profit departments. It was a gamble, but it was essential. Competition in them was so keen from more specialized rivals, their annual turnover was so meager and their potential at Macy so limited, that they could be lopped off despite the complaints from loyal Macy customers. So pharmaceuticals went, as did major appliances, sporting goods, toys, a number of more commodity-type apparel departments, and, most strategically, the bargain basements.

One more ingredient was needed and he had been determinedly working on it—his new team. He already had the continuing support of his old cronies, Mark Handler, Arthur Reiner, the two Friedmans, Herb and Bob, Phil Schlein, in the other divisions. But he would need a vital team of senior vice-presidents and vice-presidents and by working through Smiley and Herb Seegal, the corporate chairman and president, respectively, he got them. He then began a program of socializing with them, inviting them to play tennis, or to spend some hours at his new Connecticut home either at tennis or at the pool. So much could be done by getting to know your people in the off-hours, and he enjoyed their company, feeling he could invigorate them and they would invigorate him.

Gradually, as 1974 drew to an end, he was putting into effect all the elements of his plan. And it wasn't so much a complaint as a challenge when he growled to his team, "I'm sick and tired of hearing about Bloomie's! Aren't you sick and tired of hearing about Bloomie's?"

In the year that followed, the wealth of actions that Macy's took made things seem at times like a blur. The store in the Roosevelt Field Shopping Center lost its bargain basement in favor of a linens-and-domestics department, expanded to double its prior upstairs space. This was the first step in the program to give up all the traditional, low-price basements. Plans were made to devote the subsurface level at Herald Square to a large housewares department, but Finkelstein was toying with the idea of expanding it on the lines of "The Cellar" at the Union Square store in San Francisco.

Other traditional department stores, such as Marshall Field in Chicago and Gimbels in New York, however, were still committed to the budget basement. It was a crowd-puller and also tapped a segment of the public that didn't ordinarily shop in the same stores' upstairs departments. The most famous "basement" of all was, of course, the Filene's Bargain Basement in Boston and its branch stores. Their automatic markdowns, based on specific periods after the goods were first put on sale, were widely respected and had spawned a number of imitators. But Finkelstein had other ideas.

"I don't feel that budget sections have to be in the basement—they can be upstairs, too," he told *The New York Times* in an interview in March 1975. "We believe we are a value store on all floors." The move took some selling on his part. Jack Straus felt that it was an integral part of Macy's great public attraction and confirmed the company's commitment to value. But his new New York chief had a fine track record and deserved support even if his idea might seem radical on the surface.

On the theory that shoppers might be wearying of traditional store hours, Finkelstein took to changing them. The flagship store, which traditionally opened for business at 9:00 A.M., tested an 8:00 A.M. opening and it appeared promising. On the opposite end, he lopped off a half hour to close the stores at 8:30 P.M. on Monday and Thursday nights. And on Fridays, in the belief that many shoppers considered the nights part of the weekend, he closed the stores at 7:00 P.M., two hours early. And on Tuesdays and Wednesdays, he extended the operations by one hour to 7:00 P.M. He explained that the moves resulted from a study that showed that the last half hour of operations on the late nights, Monday, Thursday, and Friday, weren't productive and were getting even less so. But to compensate the shopper who still wanted to shop after work, he said, he was extending the store hours somewhat on the other nights. Was it due to public fear of night crime? he was asked. "No," he said. "Just changing consumer habits."

It was, perhaps, a minor change, but Finkelstein's aggressiveness in altering the traditional schedule of store hours—his moves were later emulated by the other New York stores—presaged a more dramatic step the following year. After the state's Sunday blue laws were struck down and two discounters, Alexander's and Korvettes, took the initiative to open their doors on Sunday, Macy's became the first traditional department store to follow suit. The decision proved controversial, with the New York Archdiocese and others protesting. But in time Sunday became the second most productive day of the week—after Saturday—even though it stole some of the shopping thunder from Mondays.

And then, after a staunch presentation to the Straus–Smiley–Seegal hierarchy in the face of some determined questioning, Finkelstein wrested approval for the biggest project of all. He wanted to remodel at least 25 percent of all of the store space in the sixteen units, including that of the Herald Square store. The project would encompass seven years and would start with the Roosevelt Field store. Asked why that particular store first, he replied, with a broad smile, as if implying that he had managed a coup, "With a new basement operation, how can we leave the rest of the store untouched?"

Integral to the remodeling of Herald Square would be a belated modernization of the Macy's outmoded cash registers. All 500 would be replaced by National Cash Register 280 point-of-sale electric cash registers, which would render increased efficiency and better controls.

He sold the entire package to the thirteenth floor by declaring one principle. If all those steps were taken, he said, sales productivity of the entire division could be increased by 40 percent over the next five years. That greater sales level should yield a much better bottom line. The New York division in 1975 accounted for an impressive 38 percent of R. H. Macy's total sales of $1.4 billion, but its earnings were only the third highest of the five divisions. Was there any real question?

Go ahead, he was told.

If Finkelstein was wearying of being told that Bloomingdale's may have done "it" first or would represent the real obstacle to any Macy effort to trade up, there was no doubt in the mid-1970s that his counterpart at Bloomie's was beginning to feel the same way about Macy's.

Marvin S. Traub was something of a phenomenon, both as a retailer and human being. His mild manner and studious appearance belied an intensity and courage that surfaced unexpectedly. After the lanky youth attended Peekskill Military Academy and spent a year at Harvard College, he enlisted in the U.S. Army and served as an infantry scout in 1942 in the European campaign. With his education—though incomplete—and family connections, he could have wangled a safer and certainly cushier job, but he didn't, electing instead to handle a dangerous combat assignment. On November 15, 1944, as an American force fanned across a field to storm Fort Jeanne d'Arc in Metz, France, he was shot. He convalesced, recovered, and continued his service until the war ended in 1945.

Returning to Harvard, he threw himself into his courses and extra-curricular activities. He served as business manager of the *Harvard Crimson*, and in 1947 he graduated magna cum laude and entered Harvard Graduate School of Business Administration. A year later, he married Lee Laufer, a pretty brunette from Hewlett Bay Park, Long Island, who had graduated from Smith College in 1947. The couple lived in nearby Arlington, Massachusetts, while Marvin continued his studies at Harvard Business School. In 1949, he graduated with honors, and took his M.B.A. and his bride to New York to seek a career.

The world seemed wide open to the bustling, intense young Traub, but he chose retailing. He was no doubt encouraged to do so by his mother, Bea, who already had a successful career for a dozen years as one of Bonwit Teller's personal shoppers and supersaleswomen. Marvin's first job was at Alexander's, where he stayed for a year before joining Macy's executive training squad. He was one of a horde of Harvard M.B.A.'s who streamed into Macy in those years. Had he stayed and demonstrated anything like the skill and creativity he did later, it is interesting to ponder whether Finkelstein and Traub might not have become zealous competitors within the same organization or how this might have affected Finkelstein's career. But, in 1950, excited by what Jed Davidson and Jim Schoff had wrought at Bloomingdale's, Marvin Traub joined the uptown organization.

His first job was that of assistant to Frank Chase, the vice-president for basement operations. The rapid flow of change, the excitement of tapping new trends even before the most fashionable consumers could sense them, and the feisty youthful environment in the store delighted Traub. He threw himself into the continuous challenges these created, sometimes seeming more eager and intent than fully collected. In fact, though his devotion and rapid-fire ideas brought him increasing recognition and advancement, he never quite lost the aspect of an impetuous boyishness. In 1956, he earned his first major advancement and became divisional home-furnishings manager at the age of thirty-one, a stunning example of recognition of a young man. His rise then was rapid to vice-president, senior vice-president, and then executive vice-president. In 1969, at age forty-four, he was elected president, the number-two man behind Lawrence Lachman, the fifty-three-year-old chairman and chief executive officer who had a financial and operations background.

The Lachman-Traub management tandem, reflecting the policy of parent company Federated Department Stores to maintain its store divisions with a dual management, did not mesh especially well. The combination of the austere, restrained Lachman, whose preservation of personal dignity appeared vital to him, and the dashing, effervescent Traub, who often seemed at sixes and sevens, was not destined to be a happy one. Under the paternal wing of Harold Krensky, the Federated group vice-president and former Bloomie's chairman, the pair got along on the surface and worked well in the exploitation of Bloomingdale's innovative policy, but it was a nervous relationship.

Krensky, a former newspaperman, advertising manager, and a freewheeling type himself, did not mind spiking the dignity of his division chiefs when he thought it was necessary. One day he came into Bloomingdale's during the busy Christmas season and was dismayed to find a line of women gathered at the cosmetics counter to be waited on. Obviously, management was too busy or diverted to be conscious of the delay at the main floor cosmetics counter.

Getting on the house phone, Krensky dialed Traub's direct line. When Marvin answered, Krensky demanded, "Marvin, what are you doing right now?"

"I'm getting rid of some paperwork, Harold."

"Paperwork—in the middle of the Christmas season?"

"Certainly—"

"Marvin, do you know there's a bunch of women can't get waited on at the cosmetics counter? Get your ass down here and help out!"

Traub dropped everything and ran.

In the early and mid-1970s, Bloomingdale's fortunes soared as the Upper East Side of Manhattan flourished with the growth of high-priced, high-rise apartments, the increase in two-income, professional families, and the influx of foreign tourists. Many of those consumers wanted more than a taste of the better life, a sense of belonging to the best of New York, and craved their share of the glamour of the international scene. It wasn't just narcissism but a desire to enjoy the fruits of what they had earned. Many had risen from modest circumstances, whether it was a ghetto in the Bronx or Chicago or the wrong side of the Seine in Paris or Florence. Now *nouveaux riches*, their homes, personal grooming, leisure-time enjoyment, and travel were a measure of their achievements. Bloomingdale's sharpening awareness of its role as the "store like no other in the world" served that craving and its fortunes reflected it.

It was hardly an accident. The Davidson-Schoff team, those émigrés from Macy's, had launched that policy with their shift from a Gimbels-type, promotional approach to a massive capitalization of the Henri Bendel, forward fashion concept. Krensky, promoted by Federated in 1966 from the chairmanship of its Boston division—Filene's—to the same post at Bloomingdale's, continued that march up the glamour path by hiring Katie Murphy, a much-respected fashion coordinator, from Bonwit Teller. As Bloomie's vice-president and ready-to-wear fashion director, she was obligated to pinpoint burgeoning fashion influences and instruct buyers on how to capitalize upon them. Starting in 1967, she began operating on the basis that a goodly portion of those upwardly mobile customers knew in general what they wanted but not in specifics. Bloomingdale's had to show them not only by its choice of special goods but with a presentation that excited their senses and inflamed their emotions. Her approach was to present showcase boutiques of European designers and in the process imbue those shops-within-a-shop with the authentic flavor of famous fashion streets in Paris, Rome, and Florence. In 1968, the first of these boutiques, known as Mic Mac, featured the large coats of Michael and Chantal Faure of Saint-Tropez. Boutiques by such other designers as Yves St. Laurent and Halston followed. Each succeeded beyond Bloomingdale's expectations.

Murphy, the fashion doyenne, also confirmed Krensky's confidence in two other ways. With her warmth and sensitivity, she encouraged more obscure apparel makers by promising them guaranteed minimum orders for the right to allow Bloomingdale's to design their lines and keep them exclusive to itself. Bloomie's, in turn, would hire as yet unrecognized design talent to make the samples. The result was a constant flow of fresh collections that Bloomie's could feed into its expanding aisles of boutiques or into its regular ready-to-wear departments. In addition, fulfilling her role of a fashion impresario who could stage a full, coordinated fashion image throughout an entire store, she was able to inspire new, young buyers to cooperate and to foster the talents of fledgling stylists. Soon, Bloomingdale's reverberated to "fashion excitement," a term that Marvin Traub dearly clasped to his bosom, and the top and bottom lines of its balance sheet glowed.

Traub added to Bloomie's boom in his own way. His eagerness, his zest for change, and his endless flow of ideas motivated the buyers and merchandisers. He was the type of executive who could emit twenty ideas in a day rapid-fire fashion and be happy if only one or two clicked. Not only was that a good average, but it also built a climate of innovativeness among the younger executives. Although he had a background in home furnishings dating from his first few posts at Bloomie's, he also threw himself into the apparel and other soft-lines fashion business, learning as he hurled ideas at wide-eyed merchandisers. And he began, with two-week, lightning visits to other countries, to think of expanding Bloomingdale's policy of holding import or international fairs to make them grander in scale.

He also often visited Bloomie's branch stores in Stamford, Connecticut; in North Bergen and Short Hills, New Jersey; Fresh Meadows in Queens; and New Rochelle, New York. Traub told store managers and department managers there that he realized that they often felt left out, remote from the Manhattan headquarters, and he meant to enhance their roles and give them strength and identity to their stores. They would in due course share in the "fashion excitement" of the Fifty-ninth Street store because "there are Bloomie's customers everywhere." And he let them in on the secret that he meant to locate Bloomie's stores all over the country—in Boston, Philadelphia, Washington, D.C., Chicago, the upper Midwest and, who knows, maybe California.

Who was the Bloomie's customer? He equated them with "young thinking people," in a 1970 interview with Paul Hanenberg in *Women's Wear Daily.* These are "people who are not necessarily young in age, but adventurous in living and who think young, who are knowledgeable, who have taste—perhaps more taste than income and people who don't necessarily live on Park or Fifth Avenue," Traub said.

"We're not pitched to Park Avenue or Fifth Avenue trade in our fashion excitement. We're shooting for a Bloomingdale's universality, whether it is in men's furnishings, men's wear, women's fashions, or home furnishings and we're going on the basis proved by our experience and success that we can create fashion excitement in every area of satisfying customers' wants and needs in excitement," said Traub.

And by 1973, when Ed Finkelstein sat down in his new seat at

Macy's Herald Square, Marvin Traub, king of fashion excitement, was clearly his archrival. A face-off between the two was inevitable.

They were similar in a number of ways. Both were graduates of Harvard College and the Harvard Business School. Both had elected retailing for their career businesses. Each had three children; each had a son named Robert; and each had a seriously ill child.

They were both aggressive toward suppliers, extremely competitive toward rivals and difficult, often truculent toward the media. Traub seemed to feel that newspapers should publish only favorable news about retailers and not probe much beyond the publicity releases. And Finkelstein was defensive, suspicious, and sensitive toward any negative nuances published about him or Macy.

Once when I was talking to Traub about business in a brief telephone interview, I asked him, "Why was business last month only so-so, Marvin?"

"Why?" he repeated.

"Yes, why?"

"Ike, why do you always ask me why?"

"Because that's one of the main things our readers like to know— why things happen."

"Well, don't ask me why. I don't know why."

In the case of Finkelstein, I had been introduced to him shortly after he had returned to New York. When I entered an elevator at the Penn-Statler Hotel (later to be called The Penta) to attend a Macy stockholders' meeting, there he was, surrounded by a group of close associates, including Arthur Reiner, Bobby Friedman, and others. Finkelstein and I nodded to one another. As I turned to face the front of the elevator, I noticed that Finkelstein lifted a finger to his lips to motion silence to the others while the elevator ascended.

But, in other ways, their personalities couldn't have been more diverse. Finkelstein was controlled, confident, calculating but smooth. Traub was more openly natural, eager, and friendly. Both were highly regarded by their peers and by suppliers but in subtly different ways. Traub had enhanced an already successful policy and was therefore not considered as much a pioneer. Finkelstein had inherited a difficult situation in the Macy New York division and had to sink or swim with an entire new program. As people began to talk about a potential Macy turnaround, Traub had to sit up and take notice. And as Macy's fortunes improved, Traub began to feel a new pressure.

But during the course of the 1970s it didn't much matter. Bloomie's and Traub, who later succeeded to the chairmanship, were in the catbird seat. They had already done all the right things—the trading up to the "young thinking" shoppers, the widespread use of in-store boutiques, and the application of visual merchandising. These and other innovations were being tested by Finkelstein and had yet to deliver in the measure that they had for Bloomie's. One of the problems was the difference in the location. Herald Square, a mass transit hub, was a center of moderate-income commuters, while Fifty-ninth Street and Lexington Avenue drew a higher-income customer, largely from affluent Park Avenue but also from other boroughs and counties. Bloomie's, in other words, was already a "destination" store before that goal became an optimum one in retailing a decade or so later. One could argue that Macy's Herald Square was, too, but its focus and therefore attraction were to the less well-heeled consumer.

Finkelstein, it was obvious, would have to carry the fight against some difficult odds on an uncertain terrain.

CHAPTER SEVEN

CATCHING UP
TO LEAD THE PACK

A haven of confident dignity, Macy's senior executive floor had a deceptively quiet look. The phlegmatic security guard, the beige expanse of carpeting, the long, open corridor with offices on the left, and only a pair of sofas and soft chairs to receive the visitors to the entire bank of offices presented an island of calm in a troubled sea. In 1975, dwindling finances and great debt had thrown New York City to the brink of bankruptcy; unemployment was mounting; street crime was inching up again. Corporations threatened to depart for more solvent shores and safer neighborhoods—and retail sales wilted.

But in the staid hush of the thirteenth floor, Jack Straus pervaded, his aristocratic presence felt even though he was frequently away. Only occasionally was the silence broken by the appearance of a discreet secretary or a preoccupied executive. To a curious visitor, it resembled an empty stage with the action presumably going on in the wings.

In the first office, Donald B. Smiley, corporate chairman and chief executive, sat stolidly. A lawyer and son of an Iowa storekeeper, he oversaw the company's finances, the vast administrative and operational activities of seventy-six department stores from one coast to the other. A man coolly comfortable with merchants and nonmerchants alike, he had undeniable management talents. But his measured temperament kept him more respected, even admired, than he was liked. He kept his own counsel, always the loner.

In the next office, Herbert Seegal, a Bostonian transplanted first to Richmond, then to Newark and New York, seemed a model of reserve. Both Smiley and Seegal were in the Straus mode, but Seegal, the corporate president, was liked. His hesitant smile had a warmth and softness that removed the barrier that a company's chief merchandiser ordinarily would erect. His role was essentially both creative and corrective, but he conducted himself basically as a teacher, demanding albeit understanding. Yet, he, too, was a loner.

The odd combination of two loners working together created a coolness, sometimes an iciness, at the top, which all Macyites felt in the lower strata. But it also built a reserve between the two men that was rarely broken.

Down the hall in the New York chief executive's office, Ed Finkelstein smoked a cigar at his desk. Behind him were photographs of his mother, one of his sons, another of his wife, and a framed tearsheet of one of his promotions with a photo of himself when he had been forty pounds lighter, more dour, more hungry, and more driven. In recent years, he had put on a milder mien and much weight, the latter partly because he had taken to inveterate candy-noshing.

Despite the calm and undisturbed quiet on the thirteenth floor, much was going on at Macy's. Seegal finally had become corporate president and in effect chief merchant in 1972 after his archrival, Dave Yunich, resigned as vice-chairman to become chairman of the Metropolitan Transit Authority, the city's transportation agency, and after Ernest Molloy had retired as corporate president. As co-vice-chairman with Yunich, Seegal had chafed at the bit in a nonstrategic role. Jack Straus, though retired in 1968, still called many of the shots on the board and chose to place the two rivals in an equal status so that one wouldn't be favored over the other. Yunich had steadily lost standing with Straus over the former ballplayer's charismatic behavior. He was too prominent in community and charitable activities, violating a Straus dictum that Macy executives stay close to the business and let him have the outside exposure. The choice of Molloy, a capable operations man, as president was Straus's way of rapping Yunich's wrist. And, in the process, Seegal's was rapped, too.

Now Seegal was where he wanted to be and he made the most of it. Within eighteen months, he had deployed five of the brightest younger men he had developed to head up most of the store divisions. So

Ed Finkelstein sat at the head of the New York division, Mark Handler in Bamberger's, Herbert Friedman in Atlanta, Phil Schlein in San Francisco, and Leslie Ball in Kansas City. Everyone assumed that all would function in the Seegal style and implement his philosophy. That meant simply test and retest departmental performance; increase sales productivity through the realignment of departments, shifting of merchandise concepts, or personnel; and keep opening new stores in existing Macy markets, ever widening their radius.

Only months after his arrival in New York, Finkelstein made it clear that he wouldn't be a Seegal clone. He would adopt the substance of his mentor's credo but he would refine the concept according to his own experience. In an interview, he said, "Herb Seegal has been a major influence on my merchandising life. But I spent fourteen years at Macy's New York before I went to Bam's and then to California. So I understood the New York operation, too, before I went anywhere else. What we want to do now is to install the same methods and systems in New York that worked in New Jersey and California. These are both also highly competitive markets and there is no reason why the same methods can't work here."

Seegal, knowing by now that his prize pupil had an independent streak, was undaunted by such comments. Soon after, he would see it dramatically when Finkelstein told Smiley that he would leave Macy if Seegal continued to snap at his heels. Smiley, in the middle, stepped into the breach with a soothing comment. Referring directly to the new, senior organization that he and Seegal headed and obviously defending the latter, he asserted, "In our merchandising efforts, we have a cohesiveness among our merchants that we haven't had before and the result is that approaches and merchandising philosophy have stabilized."

Pushed by Seegal, a program was generated to loosen Macy's concentration on household durables, a merchandise category most pressured by competition from Korvettes, Sears, and local department stores, and to give greater priority to apparel and other soft lines in order to boost profits. In the last five years, Smiley affirmed, "Our soft lines' percentage of total sales has moved from 55 percent to 63 percent. This is by and large the profitable part of the business. You get better margins and higher inventory turnover from it."

In lieu of the discontinued departments, a number of remaining departments had been given new clout, more inventory, additional brands, and improved presentation. Linens and domestics were one and their revitalized sales and profits harked back to Finkelstein's first buyer's job when he had been given that department and earned his spurs there. But other departments, such as furniture and floor coverings, men's wear, and jewelry were also highlighted in similar manner. The moral was that if one can make new strides with one part of the business, it's likely that it can be done with others if they could also demonstrate the same new life signs.

"The Cellar," that airy series of housewares and food enclaves in the basement, had generated much attention, especially among young married and professional singles. But more refinements were needed and scarcely a day went by in which Finkelstein didn't show up there, watch what people bought or didn't buy, and discuss it with department managers. Besides the Roosevelt Field store, other Macy branches had installations of "The Cellar" and the same excitement was noted.

And then there was the Christmas dilemma.

It was something that had troubled others long before Finkelstein's arrival. Given the proposition that the period between the day after Thanksgiving Day and December 25 can deliver as much as 30 percent of all annual sales and as much as 50 percent of annual profits, why, everyone wondered, was it that those boons did not accrue at Macy in that season? There were lots of theories. Macy did not have the glamour to draw the better-gift buyers. Macy was seen as just another, middle-price store, a cut perhaps above nearby Gimbels, but not in the same fast league as Bloomingdale's, or Saks Fifth Avenue, or Henri Bendel. You don't come to Macy's to buy gifts—you come there to buy necessities. And so on.

In 1976, Finkelstein took a big step to capture Macy's rightful share of the Christmas pie. All of the New York division's sixteen stores, with their collected mass of six million square feet, were promoted as never before as the "Christmas store—the big gift stores." Six key merchandise areas, all deemed to be natural categories for gift-giving, were selected as the target battle zones. In extensive newspaper advertising, on radio, television, and in catalogs and other direct mail, New Yorkers were treated to the aesthetics, appeal, and emotional values of apparel, women's accessories, china and glassware, housewares, gourmet foods, and linens and domestics. All that drive, expense, and effort gave Macy's New York its biggest December in history and the largest gain in Christmas sales in the area.

But a good part of those big pluses also came from the first Sunday openings at Macy's. After Alexander's and Korvettes had first opened their doors on that day, other stores, especially those on Fifth Avenue, Madison, and Lexington Avenue, had followed with apparent reluctance. But Macy's had sensed that the two discounters had latched on to an idea whose time had come, and Finkelstein blithely brushed off annoyed complaints from some church and consumer groups, particularly the New York Archdiocese. The validity of the move came quickly. At first merely curious, consumers soon flocked to stores on Sunday. Promptly, Finkelstein labeled Sunday business as the second-best of the week after Saturday.

Nonetheless, the Sunday openings remained controversial. Macy's competition, especially Bloomie's, perhaps the archrival, fought hard to reinstitute the Sunday blue laws through the legislature. The store opponents disliked the extra costs of the Sunday operations and the staff dislocations and inwardly quailed at the charges of religious desecration. Early in 1977, two new bills to cancel seven-day-a-week store operations awaited Governor Hugh Carey's signature, but the hand of the New York governor seemed to be stilled as lobbying groups for and against the Sunday business milled around his office and in the state houses in Albany.

It was all paying off for Finkelstein and Macy's. The December and Christmas gains proved to be the cherry on top of the whipped cream. The revived results at the New York division—a several-hundred-fold jump on prior-year earnings—paced Macy's corporate boom to 12.8 percent higher sales in the fiscal quarter ended April 30, 1977, and nine times higher net income. Earnings per share jumped from 2 cents in the year-earlier quarter to 31 cents in the latest period. And for the cumulative nine months, the glow was even brighter—a 20 percent increase in earnings.

Proudly, Mortimer Levitt, R. H. Macy's senior vice-president for finance and administration, declared, "Our merchandising and new stores have all begun to sing, with the major improvement in the New York store operations, plus a 5 percent gain in Macy's New York as a result of Sunday openings which began here at the end of last August."

Macy's gains contrasted sharply with those of two close rivals. In the same quarter, Federated Department Stores, the largest department store chain, with divisions such as Bloomingdale's, Abraham & Straus, Filene's, and I. Magnin, suffered a 4.5 percent drop in earnings. And the May Department Stores Company, operating such stores as G. Fox in Hartford, the Hecht Company in Washington, D.C., and Baltimore,

and Famous-Barr in St. Louis, fell 11.3 percent in its quarterly earnings. Of course, Macy's was comparing its results with depressed year-
earlier sales and profits, but all retailers were facing reluctant shoppers
hung up on double-digit inflation, the highest in years. And so Macy's
coup seemed all the more decisive.

Wall Street securities analysts reacted enthusiastically.

"Particularly strong sales gains in the Macy's New York and California divisions produced significant year-to-year improvement in
profits," declared Jeffrey Steiner and Fran Blechman of Merrill Lynch.
"Gains in comparable-store sales were particularly strong and provided sufficient leverage to offset inflationary pressures on most operating costs. The selling, general and administrative expense-to-sales
ratio was an estimated 0.7 percentage points lower year to year," they
told *The New York Times* in July 1977.

Walter F. Loeb, the former Macyite who had become a retailing
analyst at Morgan Stanley & Company, observed in the same *Times*
article, "It takes a long time for customers to be reeducated and
sometimes that needs a charismatic type of event. This is especially
true with the sophisticated shopper. Macy's did it with 'The Cellar,' its
first-floor boutiques, and its new sixth floor linens and domestics section. All that created new excitement, a new presentation and, in fact,
the development of a new franchise with the public."

And what did Bloomie's think? A decade and a half earlier, the
uptown store had also undergone a thorough swing from promotion to
innovation, blunting the competition from the other stores, including
Macy's. Perhaps, just perhaps, the shoe might be beginning to pinch at
Bloomie's.

"No doubt about it, Macy's has done a remarkable job, but they
certainly haven't done what we have, nor have they stolen away our
customers," said a Bloomingdale's executive who asked not to be
identified. "They've traded up, but they haven't been able to corral the
Upper East Siders down there, and they haven't gotten the affluent
shoppers to come down en masse, either. What they have actually
done is to more successfully entrench themselves in the middle-
income market."

Nonetheless, in the face of this success there were some disquieting
elements knocking—if faintly—at that quiet oasis of the thirteenth
floor.

Bank credit cards, the newest plastic in a field dominated by the travel-and-entertainment cards, were slowly cutting a swath through traditional retailing, having already been quickly accepted by the discounters. Macy's remained adamant against the bank cards; it wanted only its own credit cards, although it might honor the T&E cards such as American Express or Diner's Club.

Macy's spent good sums modernizing its old credit operations, but this didn't extend to credit cards. Explained Don Smiley, "We want to deal with our customers not through someone else's services." Macy's, in other words, wanted to maintain control of its charge customers for both merchandising and promotional purposes. It could massage the data derived from sales and demographic records and pinpoint its promotions to specific customer segments. And, in the process, it could save the fees it would have to pay for bank credit cards. But the steadfast policy against bank cards tended to reinforce consumer and trade claims that Macy's was still pretty much old-fashioned despite the changes it had made.

Another contentious matter was Macy's lack of diversity. It was the pure department store company, the most undiversified retailer among the big chains. Federated, Dayton Hudson, Carter Hawley Hale, Associated Dry Goods, and Allied Stores had specialty stores, narrow but deep in a particular type of goods. And the other major department store chains such as May had additional retail formats, such as discount stores or shoe stores. The only other "pure" department store operator was Mercantile, but its policy of locating itself in smaller cities or larger ones where it could be the dominant retailer was a particular one that none of the others chose to follow.

After Herb Seegal had made an abortive effort to buy Neiman-Marcus, the Dallas fashion chain, and an unsuccessful foray into furniture warehouse showrooms with the small J. Homestock stores (later sold to Levitz Furniture), Macy's seemed to give up on diversifying. Was Macy's again hiding in a cave of its own making? Finkelstein, for one, didn't think so: "We continue to think that the department store format is the most viable." But a decade later, when Macy's finally announced its entry into several series of specialty shops and the story by this writer noted that the venture was "a belated one," Finkelstein bristled. It wasn't a matter of being "early or late," he told a press meeting, but of "being right."

Another element that bothered Smiley and Seegal, but naturally not Finkelstein, were growing reports in 1976 and 1977 that the success of the New York chairman was creating a growing market for him at other companies. Rumors surfaced that he was being eyed and was receiving feelers from Federated, Dayton Hudson, and the Batus Retail Group, owned by British-American Tobacco Company, Ltd., for its Marshall Field division in Chicago. For Finkelstein, the demand for his services at substantially higher salary than his $300,000 a year was obviously gratifying. Jack Straus, still a major power at Macy's, didn't like it, protesting that any executive who had been invested with considerable advancement owed the company loyalty above all. But Smiley and Seegal, already well schooled in the cannibalistic nature of American retailing, were more practical about it. They had recognized the need to keep the brilliant executive happy, giving him a low-interest loan to buy a New York apartment when he returned to New York. That apartment cost the company about $15,000 a year in contrast with Smiley's own apartment, which had a $5,000 rental. Asked why a division head had a more lavish apartment than the corporate chief executive, Smiley explained that "Mr. Finkelstein has much more entertaining to do."

But they knew that the strides that Finkelstein, as well as his colleagues, made had a reverse side—the possibility that he or any one of them might carry their talents elsewhere for the right inducements. Ironically, Finkelstein, too, had the same fears of desertion by his own team, and from them he demanded and exacted promises of personal loyalty.

On June 13, 1978, Ed Finkelstein was promoted from president to chairman of Macy's New York and chief operating officer. Soon after, he was also named chief executive officer. It was high recognition of his work at age fifty-three. And it put him directly in line for succession to the very top of the corporation, which was expected to take place at the annual shareholders' meeting in November of the following year, when both Smiley and Seegal, each sixty-five years old, were expected to retire from the company.

But within Finkelstein's elevation to the New York division's top posts was another story. While Finkelstein was still in California, the Smiley–Seegal team promoted Ronald Seltzer and Stanley Abelson, two career Macyites, to run the New York division. Seltzer, who was a skilled operations man, became chairman and Abelson, an experienced merchant, was named president. Both were well respected by Herb Seegal, but when Finkelstein was brought back to New York, he displaced Abelson, who was named an executive vice-president. Dis-

mayed by the change, Abelson soon after left Macy to become president of Gimbels Philadelphia, a lesser post in a smaller division but
one in which he could run his own show.

That left Finkelstein nominally the number-two man in the division
under Seltzer. But the two big egos jostled one another. Seltzer,
respected as an excellent administrator who was also known for his
total recall of big events and small details, soon found himself crowded
by Finkelstein at almost every turn. And when Finkelstein in 1978
became division chairman, Ron Seltzer, like Abelson, was downgraded
to executive vice-president of operations. In effect, said a close Finkelstein associate who declines to be named, "Ron became a sort of
building superintendent, certainly a ridiculous role for a guy who ran
the whole division." In due course, Seltzer left for a more lucrative,
more rewarding role at Lionel Inc.

And so by summer of 1978, Finkelstein had Macy's biggest, most
important division in the palm of his hand. Two of his closest associates
were posted in key, related jobs: Arthur Reiner was appointed president of the division and Bob Friedman became its executive vice-
president for ready-to-wear apparel and accessories. Mark Handler,
Finkelstein's best friend and intimate, ran Bamberger's. Herb Friedman was the man at Davison's, the Atlanta division, and Phil Schlein
headed the California stores. Not only was New York in hand, but the
team was now deployed in all the most strategic, most potent positions.

Macy's, Herald Square, New York (*Karen Halverson/NYT Pictures*).

Jack I. Straus—"Mr. Jack"—at Macy's in the 1960s (*NYT Pictures*).

Kenneth H. Straus in 1963
(*NYT Pictures*).

David L. Yunich (*Neal Boenzi/NYT Pictures*).

Herbert L. Seegal and Donald B. Smiley (*Jack Manning/NYT Pictures*).

Herbert Friedman joined Macy's in 1950; by 1966
he was senior vice president of Bamberger's New
Jersey. He later became chairman of Macy's Atlanta
division (*NYT Pictures*).

Marvin Traub of Bloomingdale's, one of the first to use show-business techniques to actively pursue the consumer (*NYT Pictures*).

Arthur Reiner, successor to
Edward Finkelstein as chairman
and chief executive of Macy's New
York division (*NYT Pictures*).

Robert Friedman, chairman of
Bamberger's New Jersey division
(*NYT Pictures*).

"The Cellar" at Macy's (*Jack Manning/NYT Pictures*).

Edward S. Finkelstein, Macy's chairman and engineer of the $3.7 billion management buyout in 1985 (*Phil Huber/NYT Pictures*).

Mark Handler, Macy's president, and Edward Finkelstein after the company's 1984
annual meeting (*Edward Hausner/NYT Pictures*).

CHAPTER EIGHT

SUCCESS, THE BIGGEST COMPETITOR

Between August 1, 1979, and through most of 1985, few merchants, nor indeed any American business executive, were as lavishly praised as Ed Finkelstein. He basked in accolades from the media, Wall Street, academia, management organizations, and his peers, even his rivals. He was the newest example of the indigenous, American boy-grown-man who had wrested a tired organization, one that otherwise might well have gone down the drain or been submerged under the grasp of a more acquisitive company, and transformed it into a highly profitable winner through the exercise of an agile mind, hard work, and the skill to motivate others. He was a stunning role model for other middle-aged executives struggling to convince their managements of their turnaround plans or grappling with their own trauma of self-doubt and perhaps their erosion of skills.

Even other merchants who were cool to his cautious reaction to them, sensing that one with his combination of ego and proven accomplishment couldn't just warm to everyone, agreed that his achievements were of major proportions. Joseph E. Brooks, no mean merchant himself, who had made a major breakthrough at another old, traditional retailer, Lord & Taylor, observed in 1983, "Macy has done an excellent job of positioning itself as an important, upscale, quality mass marketer. This is how I perceive Ed Finkelstein's strategy and he has done it very well by giving all of his stores a particular point of view."

There was even a refreshing dimension to his achievement. Nothing is more inspiring or worthy of recognition than new, invigorating life breathed into a staggering, doddering institution or culture. On different scales, John F. Kennedy had done it for American pride. Later, Peter Ueberroth would do it for the Olympics. Lee Iacocca would do it for Chrysler Corporation.

Indeed, many referred to Finkelstein's accomplishment as "The Macy Miracle." The fact was that everything that he did seemed to be working for him, delivering unprecedented results. Even the blips were "good" blips, dips in a curve that were no mean achievements in themselves. For example, annual sales gains against the prior years soared from 1979 through 1982—12.2 percent, 15.3 percent, 12 percent, and 21.2 percent. In that final year, Macy's corporate sales gain of 20.1 percent topped those of every major competitor. The closest two were Allied Stores, with a sales rise of 17.7 percent, and Associated Dry Goods, with a gain of 15.9 percent. And in profitability, the comparison was even more dramatic. In operating profit per square foot, Macy's had gone from $9.55 in 1979 to $11.21 in 1980 to $12.53 in 1981 to $14.71. There was no blip there, despite the somewhat lesser sales gain in 1981. In operating profit, Macy exceeded those of all of its six prime competitors.

Finkelstein, it was clear, was doing everything right, summoning up everything he had learned in New York, Newark, and San Francisco to produce the broad-scale gains for the entire company. Acting on two policies that he had espoused during the halcyon days at Bam's, he brushed aside any possible risks and pushed big inventories and unleashed even more buyers to ferret out the newest, likely hot sellers. Other merchants watched literally with open mouths as Macy's stocked its stores with what they estimated was anywhere from 10 percent to 20 percent more than the sales trend portended. Obviously, Finkelstein's strategy was to be prepared for any sales bulge, even if it wasn't merited or expected. He developed a buzzword for the concept: deliberately "distorting" the business.

And Macy's willingly absorbed the extra cost of new merchandise administrators and buyers for the possible benefits that might come from an eager young man or woman whipping through a supplier's samples collection to uncover some wonderful nuggets. Such zest, if combined with some penetrating vision, could conceivably unearth a complete new customer market or segment. Finkelstein well remembered a morning in 1970 in San Francisco when he sat in on a women's sportswear review and heard a casual comment by the buyer that made him straighten up with surprise. The discussion had begun with some concern about the future trend of junior wear due to data that showed a decline in the number of teenagers over the next few years. Petite high-school and college undergraduates were an important component of the junior size. The buyer thought a moment and observed that perhaps that would happen but there would also be a "new age segment of women who would no longer be junior-size customers but would retain a spirited outlook on their clothes and their life in general."

Finkelstein was excited by the thought. It rang true. Junior clothes weren't just a smaller size. They were also a style, a spirit, a way of life. The flesh might give but not the vivacity. The buyer's offhand comment made lots of sense to him. As he said later in an interview, "We seized on that. We saw it as a basic business opportunity, not as much as a lifestyle as on the basis of changing demographics." The immediate result was the opening of a "Young Collectors" department first in San Francisco and later in the other stores, and, indirectly, the vision of older customers thinking and living young led to the introduction of "The Cellar" with a similar pattern of introduction.

In essence, the philosophy of multiplying merchandiser and buyer layers was entrepreneurially driven. If buyers could be inspired to pragmatic creativity that could boost both sales and profits, they should also be rewarded for that with extra bonuses and advancement. The policy grew as Finkelstein moved to the corporate chief's office, backed by his enthusiasm and the successful history of such moves. Other retailers were going the other way—combining buyer assignments and putting more departments under a merchandise manager's wing. It didn't matter to Macy's. In 1975, the "Club House" higher-priced women's sportswear department in the New York stores had only one buyer. By the end of 1982, it had a vice-president, a merchandise counselor, and six buyers. Asked about the results of this unusual expansion, Herbert Yalof, president of the New York division under Art Reiner's chairmanship, replied that it had raised sales twelvefold. And that meant much higher profits.

"What we wanted was a wall-to-wall productivity," said Bob Friedman, chairman of Bam's, in an interview about the same time. "This led to a search for new opportunities. For example, we identified Liz Claiborne as a potentially important designer source for women of 25 to 40 years old with upper-middle income. Since then, our business with her has exploded."

Buyers were also shifted to other jobs so as to build their experience and make them more fully rounded executives. Under David Brown, the executive development director, the most promising were quickly singled out and their career pattern shaped accordingly. The search was launched early in the career of each buyer. Finkelstein and Reiner jointly launched a policy of lunching with every new buyer, conducting a dialogue with them on mutual goals. The aim was to clarify the individual's goals and his role in the business so as to outline each one's potential at Macy.

"Some people get worried about duplication of stocks, of buyers," Finkelstein acknowledged in an interview with this writer in 1983. "We don't worry about either. We believe that if we identify what the customer opportunities are and therefore the business opportunities and do them well and maximize them, we will carry out our objectives. Risks are always there but the important thing is the entrepreneurial consideration."

Macy's would go its own way, he clearly implied. By 1983, it was obvious that he meant what he said. All other retailers were busily beefing up their support staffs in research and strategic planning. They were also establishing firm goals for return on investment, markdown rates, and other guideposts. Macy's wasn't. It insisted on having no research staff, no strategic planners, no economists. It didn't believe in rigid rules for return on investment or in markdown percentage limits. Under Finkelstein's direction and follow-through by Mark Handler, corporate president, it pursued its game plan of heavy inventories, many buyers, and vivid store presentation. And it kept building up its executive training activity, hiring as many as three hundred a year in the bigger divisions, continuously refining the program in which 70 percent of the surviving candidates would become, as Finkelstein put it, "well-rounded, entrepreneurially minded executives."

In 1984, the smoothly functioning machine ground out the best results in Macy's century-old history. Again, the company was the stellar performer among the department store retailers, but this time only more so; its financial profile was just about perfect. Sales rose 17.2 percent to $4.065 billion from 1983's $3.468 billion, itself up 16.4 percent from the 1982 level. "Comp" stores, those units at least one year old, retailing's true measure of sales, rose 14.3 percent from 1983, only a trifle under that year's "comp"-store rise of 14.5 percent. Net income jumped 18.8 percent to $221.8 million, or $4.37 a share, from $186.7 million, or $3.72 a share. Earnings as a percentage of sales rose to 5.5 percent from 5.4 percent. The income surge meant that in each of its ninety-six stores, Macy's averaged a profit after taxes of $2.31 million. It was virtually unprecedented in the field.

The fact that all of it, with the exception of the "comp" store sales gain, was an all-time record for Macy's had a salutary effect on its stock. During that 1984 fiscal year, Macy's common stock soared, delighting shareholders. The range was from a low of $41.25 to a high of $59.50; the high was the second-best after 1983's high of $64.88, but the low was almost double the previous year's $22. What that indicated was a solid confidence among all types of investors in Macy and its programs. And stockholders showed it by increasing their investment in the company, which rose to a peak of $1.168 billion from the prior year's $971.4 million.

Again Finkelstein was hailed. Bankers, shareholders, Wall Street analysts, and financial reporters vied for his attention. Since taking over the company's helm, he had tripled its sales and quadrupled its profits. Few if any merchants had accomplished that. He bought a $15 million jet aircraft for the company, its first. Jack Straus didn't like it and said so. Macy's had never needed its own plane before. But Finkelstein was steadfast and kept the plane. He entertained increasingly at his apartment and was more affable and approachable than he had been in years.

But he hardly meant to rest on his laurels. The year before, he had obtained the board's approval for Macy's most ambitious expansion. The sum of $500 million would be spent on opening ten branch stores in the Sun Belt area, equally dispersed through Florida and Texas. There were many New York expatriates and "snowbirds" residing there to give Macy's a welcome entree into such cities as Miami, Dallas, and Houston. Those stores would be under the wing of the New York division, so that Art Reiner would be responsible. Was Finkelstein at all concerned by the fact that the Sun Belt had recently suffered economic slippage because of the lower price of oil? No, he replied, he never concerned himself with economic circumstances. A smart strategy, well implemented, would take care of any shift in the economy. He had proved that, he implied, steering Macy through the treacherous shoals of the difficult 1974–75 recession a decade earlier.

He had, indeed.

In 1985, everything fell apart.

It started innocently enough in the Christmas season of 1984—actually Macy's second-quarter, since its 1985 fiscal year started in

August—with severe price-cutting by many retailers to build up a sluggish holiday season. Inventories swelled in almost every big store and the profit line wavered with the surrender of normal profit margins to reduced prices. That wasn't much different from some earlier Christmas seasons. American shoppers wanted better values and they were beginning to suspect that "regular" prices and "suggested" retail prices were inflated in order to contain good profits. Retailers had to respond with lower prices during the season and even before. But after the Christmas results of 1984 were tallied, the worst was realized. The year-to-year sales rise for December was one of the smallest of the year, when it should have been the largest. Profits in the 1984 final quarter for most retailers whose fiscal year ended January 31 were quite disappointing.

Economists blamed much of the sour performance on a pessimistic consumer buying attitude resulting from the high federal deficit, increased personal debt (Americans had indulged in a binge of auto and appliance buying), and concern over renewed inflation and increased interest rates. But it was probably the high installment debt, up to $98 billion in 1984 from $60.5 billion in 1983 and $27.7 billion in 1982, that was the real stopper.

For Macy, what appeared to be something of a blip that Christmas season almost turned into a disaster. Finkelstein found himself resorting to drastic steps and having to swallow his earlier statements about the unimportance of economic circumstances. And the irony of it all was that the very things that had worked so well for him—"distorting the business" by building big inventories—worked painfully against him in those early months of his 1985 fiscal year. The freedom and psychological lift he, Handler, and Reiner gave the young merchandisers and buyers also resulted in bulging the stores' inventories with huge clumps of unmoving goods. The only fortuitous factors were a divisional consolidation of the Midwest stores into the Atlanta division, which saved considerable costs even though more than one hundred people lost their jobs, and a pair of forced executive resignations that appeared to place the blame not at the very top but somewhat lower down among the senior executives. The dropouts were Phil Schlein, the chairman of the Macy division, and a senior vice-president at Bam's. But even those moves weren't much compensation for what had happened.

It was as if someone had turned off the faucet. In the first quarter of August through October 1984, sales rose 8.8 percent over the year before, but net earnings dropped 26.8 percent. In the second quarter of November through January 1985, sales again advanced 11.3 percent and earnings eked out a 3.6 percent rise. The income erosion returned in the third quarter of February through April. Sales rose 5 percent, but net earnings fell 12.6 percent. But in the final quarter, Macy's results were especially disturbing. In that period from May through July 1985, Macy's sales increased 3 percent, but profits plummeted 55.4 percent. For the entire year, sales totaled $4.368 billion, up 6.4 percent, against $4.065 billion, but net income was 14.6 percent below the year before at $189.3 million against $221.8 million.

What really happened? The measures behind the figures were stark enough. The profit percentage of sales slipped in the 1985 fiscal year to 4.3 percent from 5.5 percent and 5.4 percent in the two prior years. "Comp" store sales were most disappointing, registering a gain of only 4.3 percent in contrast with gains of 14.3 percent in 1984 and 14.5 percent in 1983. What it all denoted was that many of Macy's loyal customers turned away, and that heavy stocks of goods and waves of necessary markdowns to move them out of the stores robbed Macy's of much of its vaunted profit-making ability. Earnings per share were $3.69 against $4.37 and $3.72 in the two earlier years, the latest the poorest of the three years. Nothing worked—not the glamorous trading up, the store-as-theater, or the entrepreneurial drive.

To be sure, 1985 was a difficult year for most retailers. For those on a different fiscal year, beginning February 1 and ending the following January 31 (as against Macy's August 1 through July 31), business picked up in Christmas of 1985 over the previous one enough to give them a decent year and decent profits. Dour expectations did not quite materialize and most merchants breathed easier when the year ended. But the reverse had occurred a decade earlier when big inventories and heavy price-slashing hurt industry profits. Macy's, in that first year of Finkelstein's stewardship of the corporation, did very well against the pack. It then commenced to plow ahead of them, climbing a curve that lasted for a decade. But in its 1985 fiscal year, the curve took a side road that went nowhere.

Wall Street was dismayed. The hero of the analysts had faltered, and badly at that. Not only had Macy's profit margin dipped in 1985 and its "comp" gains dropped, but return on stockholders' equity fell to 4.3 percent from 14.3 percent in 1984. They now began to scale back Macy's earnings forecasts for the succeeding quarters. It was embarrassing for some of them—and their superiors who considered Ed

Finkelstein infallible and lauded him to domestic and foreign bankers—because they had been recommending the company's stock for years. To those who had watched Macy's progress, it seemed ironic that Wall Street could so abruptly turn on a company because it had slipped one year out of eleven. But that seemed to be the fate of a leader—one stumble and the pedestal starts to shake. It was clear, too, that Macy's was a victim of its own success, finding that very success a bigger rival than Bloomie's, Saks Fifth Avenue, or the economy. Publicly, Finkelstein would only say, "That year was only the second best in our history."

Now, at Macy and among professionals and amateur observers, a greater, more intensive examination of Macy's fall followed.

Those who liked Finkelstein and his team, and there were many who did, tended to pooh-pooh the decline. His record was so good, they insisted, that a temporary fallout meant little and was to be expected. In the long run, they argued, it was probably good, because it would sharpen Ed, Mark, Art, Bobby, and Herb even more. Those who didn't like Ed and the others—although no one disliked Mark Handler, who was generally considered to be a fine, genial man without a nasty bone in his body—wondered publicly whether Macy wasn't slipping. Had Finkelstein lost his clout? Was he, like so many others, so egotistical that he had begun to believe his own press clippings? Wasn't he, maybe, passé in a dizzily changing world? These were some of the racier thoughts one heard directly from critics or overheard in the New York restaurants and coffee shops where retailers and suppliers gathered.

But, on balance, the sentiment seems to bear somewhat more heavily in favor of Finkelstein. After all, ten years of consecutive profit gains were nothing to sneeze at. The earnings decline, however, understandably aroused the Wall Street analysts, who, after an initial soft approach, took after Macy's with a vengeance, helping to send Macy's stock into a tailspin.

For example, Jeffrey B. Edelman, a well-respected analyst at Dean Witter Reynolds, wrote in an equity research advisory on Macy:

Although we had been expecting disappointing results for the July quarter, the shortfall was greater than most analysts had anticipated. . . . Fourth-quarter profits declined 45 percent to 45 cents per share from 88 cents last year. We knew it was going to be bad but it was worse than we had thought. Sales were soft, up 3.7 percent overall and 1.4 percent on a comparable-store basis, which was responsible for most of the earnings shortfall. . . . It has been difficult to come to grips with what is going on at Macy's, except that it appears the company has past [sic] the point of diminishing returns in terms of how much merchandise it can efficiently move out the door. Perhaps of equal importance is the fact that the bloated industry inventories and subsequent promotional activity, somewhat overshadowed Macy's merchandising strategy. Furthermore, perhaps the excessive markups that the company has always enjoyed on private-label merchandise appeared overpriced to the consumer. We suspect there might be some changes in the company's merchandising strategy over the longer term.

On September 9, 1985, Bernard Sosnick, another much respected analyst for L. F. Rothschild, Unterberg, Towbin, stated in a report: "The revival of sales in August brought back images of the Macy we had known before its sales began to slump in September 1984. . . . The company's total sales increases were modest at the beginning of August, but gains were in the mid-teens during the remainder of the month and into September. . . . Management is trying to maintain a reserved attitude toward the latest development and says that one month does not make a season—which unfortunately was true last year."

However, on September 18, Sosnick wrote:

Results for the July quarter (the final period of the fiscal year ended August 3, 1985) were worse than expected, as earnings per share dropped from 88 cents in 1984 to 48 cents. Throughout the quarter, sales were weaker than anticipated and increased by a meager 3.1 percent. The negative surprises that came with the earnings release yesterday were in the poor comparisons for gross margins and selling expenses. The company's strategic decision to improve sales service has been putting upward pressure on expenses for about a year, but we had thought that tighter expense controls had been imposed on non-selling expenses following the disappointing earnings in the April quarter. However, selling, general and administrative expenses rose by 20 percent in the July quarter. . . . From random comments we have heard from shoppers, poor sales service is Macy's Achilles' heel. We surmise that management is aware of this and is committed to solving the problem. Thus, sizeable increases in selling expenses are likely to continue in force during the next few quarters.

Such comments, along with negative reactions to the disappointing 1985 fiscal year, inevitably came back to the same pointed question.

Was Finkelstein slipping? Were three of four bad quarters a symptom of a loss of control? Or was he, as some devoted associates and friends claimed, a victim of his own success? It was impossible to say for sure, since, after all, it was still Macy's second-best of all years.

"Finkelstein must now realize that he isn't infallible," Jeffrey Edelman of Dean Witter Reynolds told this writer for the October 13 *Times* article. Other analysts were more caustic. "Macy's has milked its strategy. It isn't unique anymore because a lot of other department stores have stolen its ideas," declared Fred Wintzer, of Alex Brown & Son in Baltimore. That seemed to be the case. In New York, Bloomie's, Saks Fifth Avenue, and Lord & Taylor were fighting back. In Atlanta, Rich's, the Federated division there, had come alive under a new, younger management, dealing some merchandising body blows to Macy's Davison's division there. In New Jersey, Bam's was meeting some new promotional clout from Stern's, the Allied Stores' unit run by a pragmatic, hard-hitting president, Larry Stone. And in San Francisco, Dave Folkman, a former Macyite who had moved over to the enemy camp as president of the Emporium, was able to use his knowledge of Macy and of the merchandising business to turn the Emporium into a more combative rival.

There were, it developed, a variety of tatters showing through the drawn curtain at Macy's in the fall of 1985. According to a consensus of consultants and analysts, these combined to give Macy a much worse year than such other big operators as the May Department Stores Company and the Dayton Hudson Corporation.

Expenses fell out of line. During fiscal 1985, sales increased a puny 6.4 percent over the year before against 1981–84 gains of from 12.1 percent to 17.2 percent. But expenses rose 16.6 percent, or to 21.8 percent of sales, against 20.1 percent of sales in 1984 and 19.9 percent in 1983. This increased disparity in the expense-to-sales ratio—a pointed indicator of management attention—was troubling as evidence of loose control.

Implicit in this was heavy advertising and promotion spending as Finkelstein, Handler, and the division heads fought to correct erratic consumer buying. But a good part of Macy's advertising involved increased funds to capture a greater share of the youthful upscale customer—who just a year or two later would be referred to as "Yuppies"—but judging by the sales results, these didn't deliver.

A push to improve Macy's customer service—how salesclerks and department managers treated shoppers—also resulted in higher costs.

Millions of dollars were put into the effort to inject some interest among sometimes indolent and disinterested co-workers. Training sessions with follow-up training sessions were part of this program, along with the offer of incentives. This move, considered belated by rivals, may have arisen from many consumer complaints that Macy clerks were unresponsive and disinterested.

Bulging inventories were obviously the main symptom of Macy's so-so sales. But the deliberate "distorting" of inventories had gone awry even before the 1985 fiscal year began in August 1984. In January of 1984, inventories were running 35 percent higher than in January 1983. Alarmed, Macy's top executives took steps to bring it under control, so by July 1985, merchandise stocks had been cut to 9.5 percent over the prior July, still a high level, but well within Finkelstein's policy of inflating inventories in the event of a sudden sales splurge. But when that splurge failed to materialize as 1985 progressed, a sense of panic set in. The shift to smaller but more frequent orders and changes in suppliers hadn't prevented stocks from overflowing. Each division was ordered to clear stocks quickly by cutting prices and advertising them heavily. Macy stores those days seemed to be "giving everything away," judging by all the "sale" signs and the added price cuts at the cash register. In a way, it was like a dam where the water level is kept high in case there is a shortage. Only instead of a drought, the skies opened up with a continuous downpour. But Macy's efforts to trim the "water level"—in the form of the aggressive price-cutting—didn't succeed, adding to the expense structure and biting sharply into profits.

Allied to this problem was Macy's private-label program. Finkelstein was sure store labels would give him better markups and help circumvent the rampant price-cutting of national brands that had already prompted him to discontinue Levi Strauss, the premier brand in jeans. Finkelstein had gone all the way with the program. He increased the Hong Kong foreign buying office, giving his son, Mitchell, complete authority there, and opened a New York operation with cutters and sewers to prepare samples emulating the best that Seventh Avenue had to offer. These were then sent to Hong Kong to be duplicated at lower prices than the American originals. At the same time, that office and plant at One Penn Plaza, just a block from Macy's Herald Square, prepared its own styles under the direction of a team of designers. It was one of the most ambitious internal "manufacturing" setups of any American retailer. But it didn't help much when sales failed to keep up with inventory levels, and much of the unmoving stocks were those Far East goods arranged with Hong Kong and other nationals. But those who thought that Ed Finkelstein might have gotten himself into a trap with private labels apparently didn't know how determined he was. At the end of that difficult 1985, he still planned to increase Macy's ratio of private labels of total sales from that year's 15 percent to 20 percent to as much as 30 percent in 1986. The trick, which he well realized, was to price them better, lower than higher, to regain errant customer loyalty.

Another disappointment was the role of household durables, ordinarily a sizable contributor to sales and profits. Stubbornly and probably to his credit, since he believed that department store customers wanted big-ticket durables as well as clothing and electronics, Finkelstein stayed with furniture and carpeting long after other competitors dropped them. But, in 1985, that didn't help, either. "Macy's, which has always been a strong durables merchandiser, didn't downplay such big-ticket goods as floor coverings and furniture in the last few years as most other department stores did," observed Herbert Wittkin, a New York retailing consultant who had been president of Stern's in New Jersey and group senior vice-president of Allied Stores' eastern stores. "But when the Reagan recovery lost momentum, the biggest letdown was in home furnishings, and this worked greatly to Macy's disadvantage, since hard lines' business is more important to them than to other department stores."

As Finkelstein put the pressure on his executives, the slow turnover of Macyites shifted into a different gear. Executives who wouldn't return calls from recruiters now not only did so but also sought them out. Macy's "balloon payments," in which wanted executives were being offered special bonuses in each year to stay but collectible only after three years, helped only fitfully. Money wasn't everything, especially when the boss suddenly turned irascible and calls from other retailers beckoned higher titles and more money.

But of all the tatters that peeked through the tight curtain—Finkelstein in 1985 seemed to return fewer phone calls and to keep his supplier contacts much more restricted—the one that seemed so revealing was the misforecasting of his business. It seemed inconceivable that a chief executive who was so sold on his own and his staff's forecasting ability that he employed no strategic planners or economists could have so misread the consumer's intentions. "Macy kept expecting big sales increases and built its inventories accordingly," said

Jeff Edelman of Dean Witter Reynolds. "But other department stores beat them to the punch by cutting their inventories, taking markdowns and cutting prices. Macy misforecast the sales and just wasn't quick enough to adjust."

Cyrus Wilson, president of Management Horizons, a leading consulting company owned by Price Waterhouse, said, "It's been part of Macy's strategy to try to dominate the market with fashion goods in depth. But if you have that strategy, you are naturally going to be more sensitive if you don't forecast correctly. Macy's quite apparently did misread the sales trend."

Why had Finkelstein misread the American consumer, and how might his almost one hundred stores in fifteen states with some 24 million square feet of retail space be affected, not to mention his almost fifty thousand employees? No one knew until Monday, October 21, 1985. That day, he and Mark Handler announced their proposal to acquire Macy's through a leveraged buyout. It is reasonable—and probably correct—to assume that he allowed a personal ambition and all the effort needed to implement it to divert him from the changes in the market place. It is difficult, if not impossible, to satisfy two conflicting demands.

CHAPTER NINE

RIDING THE CLOUDS

The competitive pressure in that tough year of 1985 was intense, but there were two other sparks to fuel emotion in Macy's corporate offices in the Herald Square store.

One was the lure of a leveraged buyout. With as little as 10 percent personal investment, you could buy a company using its cash flow and assets as collateral. Of course, you would have to raise the financing, but if you made the inducement sweet enough, that posed no real problem. For a small investment, the Macy people could own a big share leveraged on the order of one times 50. Who could, in all absolute honesty, resist that?

The other was the takeover cloud drifting their way from the rest of the retail industry. Why should Macy continue to be immune? You had to be realistic because everyone seemed to be buying everyone else in American business.

It was the year when the incredible inventiveness of the American financial community flowered with more than $24 billion of leveraged buyouts, five times as much as only two years before. The compliant Washington administration and friendly regulatory agencies seemed to give such takeovers their blessing. While productivity, the trade balance, and the federal deficit were temporarily unmanageable, perhaps Washington believed that business consolidation could only exert a churning but positive influence on the nation's economy.

Free competition was the hard core of this attitude, but it had a built-in clinker, at least in terms of the leveraged buy out (LBO). It worked like this:

A leveraged buyout, with its large amount of debt and usual high-risk, high-yield "junk bonds," resembled a contest with at least five players, each with varying relationships to the others. There was the buying group, often including senior management of the company; the other equity investors, both large and small, whether businessmen, pension funds, insurance companies, or investment bankers; the providers of the senior debt, which included some of the latter; those who prepared the junk bond offering and also invested in the equity, which also included some of the financial institutions, and, of course, the stockholders of the company being taken private, ranging from the retired executives to rank-and-file retirees, average investors, and senior citizens. The LBO was peculiar in that it involved convincing every one of the five participants that the risk was worthwhile.

Everyone in the chain thus dangled on a rope of uncertainty, with all including the unwashed shareholder opting for high return. The sales pitch, the hype, even the con, as it was in some cases, was being passed up and down the line, with the ultimate pressure exerted at the bottom. The public shareholder could scarcely hold out, since a premium was being offered over the stock's market price, and as a group shareholders largely have been unable to organize a solid front against marshaled opponents. The clinker in the LBO was that some one of the five contestants had to be pushed to the wall, usually motivated by greed, hope, or helplessness. As subsequent events showed, it was not always the shareholder—can one really hold out if the company goes fully private?—but the others who occasionally were left permanently dangling.

There was another group strung out on that shaky line that wasn't necessarily an investor in the target company—the employees. Many eventually lost their jobs as the newly private company, run by an ownership management anxious to cut expenses, pared the company by eliminating departments entirely or cutting them and selling off assets. Though not part of the deal, the employees potentially could be the most affected.

Some of the oldest and largest American firms felt the tap of the LBO. Beatrice Foods, the world's biggest foods packager, first opposed and then agreed to an $8.4 billion takeover by Kohlberg, Kravis, Roberts & Company, a leading leveraged buyout investment company. Other Kohlberg, Kravis LBO moves included Storer Communications, with a $2.5 billion financing, and Union Texas Petroleum, $1.6 billion. Jack Eckerd Company, the large Florida drugstore chain, and SCM Corporation, the business machines producer, went into LBOs backed by Merrill Lynch for $1.6 billion and $1.3 billion financing, respectively. Levi Strauss, the nation's premier apparel-maker, went private under the auspices of the founding Haas family, which already owned some 35 percent of the public stock. Uniroyal Inc., the tire-maker, did its LBO with Clayton & Dubilier for $1 billion-plus. And Merrill Lynch provided some of the $908 million funds for the private entry of Denny's, the fast-food chain.

It was a daring, almost desperate gamble for most of the players, but each had its spur. Banks, restricted by government scrutiny and the deregulation of savings-and-loan institutions, put up billions to fund takeovers, blinking at their oft-expressed reminders that they had to be basically conservative. They even participated in the equity, thus becoming participants on more than one front. Wall Street houses, eyeing heavy competition from normally staid rivals and low interest rates that reduced their former high return, not only provided some of the funds for LBOs but also started LBO funds, like mutual funds. Insurance companies, pension funds, and large private investors saw an opportunity to achieve a better return from their investments than merely through the traditional, investment vehicles. Raiders, always seeking undervalued companies, ran through the investment market, often staging threatening takeovers only to sell out their shares at a hefty profit. And a growing number of corporate managements, either fearing an unfriendly takeover offer or detecting an opportune moment, fostered an internal merger to capitalize on assets long carried on their books at lower than actual values because of traditional caution by earlier managements.

The merger arena began to resemble a circus, with various acts performing simultaneously in the big tent. One was the LBO fracas, with top executives for the first time straining to move from employees to major owners. Another was the show of the raiders, T. Boone Pickens, Carl Icahn, Irwin Jacobs, Ivan Boesky, and Ted Turner. And the third, the biggest game, which only served to inspire the others, was the megamerger. In 1985, Capital Cities Communications took over American Broadcasting Company for $3.5 billion, and the combination became Capital Cities/ABC Inc. Philip Morris Inc. acquired General Foods Corporation in a $5.6 billion deal. General Motors Corporation plunked down $5.2 billion for Hughes Aircraft Company, only a year after buying Electronic Data Systems for $2.6 billion. And R. J. Reynolds, Inc., a company that had mostly diversified out of tobacco products, paid $4.9 billion for Nabisco Brands, a major food products producer. And by year's end, in perhaps the most memorable merger, the General Electric Corporation swallowed RCA Corporation in a $6.28 billion gulp.

It was a binge in which all manner of financial institutions happily if impulsively joined. There was simply considerable capital chasing considerable opportunity. Soon, it became obvious, as the cost of mergers and LBOs rose with the growing risk, there would probably be more capital chasing less opportunity.

On the thirteenth floor of Macy's, they began to realize that the big trick in any leveraged buyout would be to maintain the payments in the financing and at the same time to make a profit. It was a contradictory process, a double-whammy that held many hazards.

The leveraged buyout—what was it but simply the latest twist, the newest mutation, the most feverish convolution to arise in the torturously aggressive mind of the American investment banker? Management and its other, friendly equity owners needed only to raise 10 percent of the total purchase price to own up to 60 percent or more of the company. The only obligations, other than the not so minor one of obtaining the necessary financing, were to have a reasonably good profit record and for the target corporation to have strong tangible assets as a form of collateral. Once approved, the buyers could then pay the principal and interest from the working capital, revenues, real estate, and other assets of the business. In the simplest terms, the major difference between a normal type of acquisition and an LBO was that the LBO group need put up only a small amount of cash and equity compared with the obligations of the regular merger or acquisition. The particular attraction that the LBO group hoped to have for those who would bankroll them was that as operating management they knew the business and were therefore best equipped to run it in a joint investment, even if the outsiders put more into it than they did. For Finkelstein, with his great repute for having turned around one of America's oldest retailers, it was perhaps the most strategic selling point.

There is contradiction about whether Finkelstein ever actually said it, putting his job on the line if the board did not accept his buyout proposal. He insisted that he had never told the directors that remaining on the job was contingent on their approval of his proposal. Others claimed that he did. But regardless, given the example of other executives at other corporations, his remaining was implicit in principle if the directors went along but highly doubtful if they didn't. He had literally saved the company. There was no gainsaying that, and that lone fact, everything else notwithstanding, gave his offer an authentic and significant imprimatur.

He had at least on one prior occasion put his job on the line with an ultimatum. It occurred in 1975, shortly after he had been elevated to president of the Macy New York division, then the largest and most troubled of the major units. Herbert L. Seegal, his mentor, had been promoted from the chairmanship of the New York division to the presidency of the R. H. Macy Corporation, running it in tandem with Donald B. Smiley, the corporate chairman and chief executive. Seegal, aware that Finkelstein had in the last few years demonstrated an increasing independence from him, nonetheless decided to ignore it and didn't hesitate to come into his protégé's office to gently chide him on some misjudgment or miscalculation or controversial move. A somber but well-intentioned and highly skilled merchant, Seegal held no rancor or jealousy toward his gifted student. But he sadly underestimated Ed Finkelstein's growing resentment of his criticism.

Irked to the extreme, Finkelstein one day walked into Smiley's office. "You know that line in the carpet that marks where the corporate offices ends and the New York division's begins?" he asked. Smiley nodded, with a slow grin. The coincidental line that a carpet-layer had created had occasioned quips more than once before. "Well," Ed said, slowly, "if Seegal crosses that line once more, I will be out of there the same day."

"Are you serious?"

"I couldn't be more serious."

Smiley nodded and Finkelstein went back to his office. From then on, Seegal never again crossed that line on his own and his relationship with Finkelstein cooled, hardened, and remained so from then on. For Finkelstein, it was a triumph of principle. But he knew he had been on safe ground. It was well known through the Macy top hierarchy that he had been offered a number of lucrative jobs by other big retail chains, including Federated Department Stores, operators of Bloomingdale's and Abraham & Straus.

As Finkelstein huddled with Mark Handler, his closest associate, and with Marvin Fenster, the attorney and corporate secretary, they decided that one of the overriding matters was that they would eventually be confronted by a takeover threat from some other company. It would probably come from another large retailer or a major shopping center building inspired by a hungry investment banker. There was already a spate of rumors that someone or some group was eyeing Federated Department Stores, the biggest of the department store chains. And with Federated probably already zeroed in by someone's periscope, could Macy's be far behind? The environment was already conducive to it, if you considered what had already happened in the retail business that year.

Mergers vied with divestitures for attention all those months. Mobil Corporation, the nation's second-largest oil refiner after Exxon Corporation, announced that it would eventually spin off its troubled Montgomery Ward division in Chicago. Ward's, founded more than a century before as the country's first important catalog sales chain, had been acquired by Mobil in the mid-1970s for some $500 million when the big oil refiner was swollen with cash over the oil squeeze of the period. But Ward's had failed to respond to the profit challenge by its new owners and the big refiner found it necessary to pump more than another $500 million into it. Now, Mobil, in announcing a potential spinoff, said that Ward's was terminating its base, the catalog business, which had sales of more than $1.5 billion. That move, plus a plan to remodel and restrategize many of the Montgomery Ward stores, was intended to spruce up Ward's profits so that it could present a brighter face and better potential investment when it would be spun off. With the growth of such aggressive retail chains as K mart Corporation, of Troy, Michigan, and of Wal-Mart Stores, of Bentonville, Arkansas, Ward's no longer seemed to have any *raison d'être* in the marketplace.

In another divestiture move, Rapid-American Corporation sold its Lerner Shops division for some $300 million to The Limited, Inc., the dynamic apparel chain operated by Leslie Wexner. And F. W. Woolworth Company, another century-old retailer, closed seventeen of its thirty-six J. Brannam off-price apparel stores, hinting that it would eventually terminate the entire loss-ridden chain, which it later did. Woolworth had leaped into the apparently lush potential market for off-price—call it "discount"—but had failed to give J. Brannam (an acronym for "Just Brand Names") any sharp focus or direction to make its mark in the stiffly competitive and rampantly expanding off-price field. Other new off-pricers also began to fall by the wayside for the same reasons or lack of real values to the consumer.

The merger front was busy, too, but not among the giants. Ames

Department Stores, a Connecticut discounter, acquired the G. C. Murphy Company, a Pennsylvania operator of discount and variety stores. Zayre Corporation, a major Massachusetts discounter, bought another discount chain, Gaylords National Corporation. And Allied Stores Corporation, a diversified retailer that had made a number of retail acquisitions in prior years, bought the Powers Dry Goods division from Associated Dry Goods Corporation. Macy's, in the view of many analysts and observers, wasn't as ripe for acquisition as either Allied or Associated Dry Goods or even the great Federated, because despite the looming profit blip that year, Macy's had a great bottom-line record for the last decade. Only those companies, big or little, with faltering or so-so profit records presented likely targets to acquirers for at least two reasons. One was that their shabby profit performance usually hurt their stock prices so that buying the company would be less expensive than buying a consistently profitable concern. Another reason was that the acquirer could and did excite investor support by promising to improve the company's management and profit and thereby its future stock values.

Nonetheless, Finkelstein professed to be nervous about a potential takeover. But, at the same time, as he talked to the experts on leveraged buyouts at Goldman Sachs & Company, he found it necessary to respond to the jabs he was beginning to get from Wall Street. It was one of those odd quirks of the big investment banking houses that their securities analysts could be involved in criticizing the performance of a client at the same time that the managing directors were talking financing to it. That sort of thing didn't happen often; Wall Street's goal was to make money, not chase it away.

"The company has been up against difficult comparisons for the last few quarters, providing for a tapering off in the rate of sales increase," observed Jeffrey B. Edelman, retailing analyst for Dean Witter Reynolds, Inc. In a brief advisory to investors on May 23, 1985, Edelman added, "Costs and expenses continue to surge ahead. One has to wonder whether they [Macy] have reached the point of diminishing return with respect to moving much more merchandise efficiently."

Still, in the view of the Macy chief, the year's dip would only be an aberration, a temporary lapse of no major proportions in Macy's upward push. It was important, he told his people, that he concentrate on the pros and cons of the leveraged buyout and not let the profit drop deter him. Yet he made it clear he wanted a better, harder-hitting performance from everyone and exhorted Mark Handler and the other top executives to make everyone toe the line and try harder.

He had done it earlier, too. The year before, when profits still seemed to be holding up despite a softening in sales, he came into his office one day in an apparent foul mood. He immediately closed his door—usually he kept it open wide, believing that it was important for everyone to see the boss on the site, working away with his hand firmly at the controls—and dictated a sharp note to his key executives. Later they privately agreed that while he always stifled any opposing views by the force of his wit, his expertise, and his self-confidence, he had evidently decided that particular day that their acquiescence and loyalty could be blunting their creativity and motivation. Was he wondering if they were just fooling him by going along to get along, losing their heart in the process, and not putting out enough?

At any rate, they were all rather startled when he informed them—by letter—that they had for quite some time enjoyed fine remuneration and perquisites but now things were going to get tougher because business had soured. They were admonished to "put your noses to the grindstone."

It was demeaning to them and uncharacteristic of him. With the economy mired in another one of its mini-recessions, business was difficult. Finkelstein had always maintained that if their strategy was right and they implemented it well, ups and downs of the economy shouldn't matter, but what was happening obviously suggested otherwise. Therefore, something had to be at fault and it must be them. But they had all been working hard and giving Macy's all they had. He had fired them up to that and nothing had really changed. Why, they wondered, did he have to put it in writing, especially when he was always so good, so convincing, and even inspiring when he spoke to them one-to-one or as a group?

But Finkelstein was especially annoyed at what he had detected as an underlying disloyalty on the part of some whom he had nurtured, developed, advanced, and enriched. Some were already showing it by leaving Macy. Of six or more who did, those who irked him most were Richard Mancuso, the financial vice-president of the Macy New York division, who left to become president of Modernage Furniture Company, a southern retail chain, and Joseph Berzok, president of the Bamberger division in New Jersey, who moved on to become vice-chairman of the Batus Retail Division, the American arm of the British-American Tobacco Company, which owned Saks Fifth Avenue, Gimbels, and Marshall Field in Chicago. Finkelstein had exploded when one of them had unloaded his bombshell in the chairman's office. He hadn't liked Berzok's departure for the competition because Berzok and Bobby Friedman, Bamberger's chairman and a particular favorite of Finkelstein's, were a good team, if not chemically always in rapport.

And then there was Philip Schlein and Frank Doroff. They hadn't left on their own initiative. Finkelstein had forced them out.

Schlein had been Finkelstein's successor at Macy's California. Finkelstein had willingly accepted the transfer to head the New York division, convinced that he had done an outstanding job in California and that he was leaving it in good hands with Schlein. Everything had gone well in California those first transition years with Finkelstein having set the pattern and the disciplined, respected Schlein faithfully adhering to it. But Schlein, it developed, had an independent streak. With northern California's economy suffering a severe erosion over the loss of aerospace and electronics contracts, retail sales in the Bay Area were hurting. With most of his competitors slashing prices and promoting heavily, Schlein didn't believe he should settle for the usual panacea when business was slipping. Macy had made great strides with its emphasis on lifestyle merchandise—the same successful pitch Finkelstein had engineered first in New Jersey and then in California on his way to repeating the feat in New York—and Phil Schlein saw no reason to depart from it. When you follow the herd, he felt, you become just another sheep.

In the frequent calls he got from Finkelstein in New York as the chairman perused the sales chart of all the divisions, Schlein began to sense that Finkelstein was becoming a bit nervous about the West Coast situation. And then, as the months progressed, Ed made it plain that he was more than concerned. He was damned worried. Even the occasional pickups in business didn't satisfy him. He didn't, he said, understand why Phil was so inflexible. But Schlein still couldn't see giving up on all that they had built so painstakingly. If Ed would be patient, they could weather the storm without losing any position. Then Finkelstein started insisting that the West Coast stores should take up the slack by increasing the emphasis on private labels, a new push that he had adopted as a way of offsetting the excessive distribution of top national brands. If properly and enthusiastically advertised, private or store labels could give a store a better markup, a semblance of exclusivity, and more flexibility than the big national brands. In the former, the retailer had the control; in the latter, the producer had it.

The private label concept was especially important to Finkelstein because he had some grand plans for it.

Schlein wasn't so inflexible as he was independent. Whether he privately resented all the accolades that Finkelstein was getting or felt that he was better in touch with the California market, he stood pat. Associates of Schlein say that his steadfastness had been supported by a very lucrative investment he had made in Apple Computer Corporation, then one of the computer industry's brightest stars. Phil had made several millions in profit on Apple and had even been invited by its management to join it in a top executive capacity. In the meantime, however, the Finkelstein-Schlein relationship soured and polarized and it was obvious to both that it could only end one way.

Neither will publicly discuss what transpired at their final meeting in New York in 1984. The reconstruction of others indicates that it involved a lengthy discussion in which Finkelstein stated his position, repeating all he wanted, and Schlein insisted that it would be wrong to shift to heavy price-cutting or to push private labels too much. Finkelstein is said to have told him that he had no choice but to insist on it and Schlein replied in kind. They stared incredulously at one another, realizing that they had come to a break after a thirty-year relationship. Schlein said he would resign and Finkelstein replied that he would have to accept it. It was a bitter moment for both, a rift both professional and personal that they knew would never be repaired.

Frank Doroff, at age thirty-three, was one of Finkelstein's young hopefuls, one of a group of about eight young men and women whom the chief executive had singled out as the smartest, the most alert, and the most promising. Others were Hal Kahn, Rosemary Bravo, and Terry Motoris, all potential divisional presidents or chairmen. Finkelstein, utilizing the sharp mind and solid instincts of David Brown, his executive development director, had discovered them, given them greater responsibility, and carefully monitored them while paying them more money than most had ever thought they would earn. As a result, he awed, frightened, and stimulated them. Yet, in warm talks with them around his pool in his Connecticut home, he also sought to engender a familial attitude among them.

Doroff, youthful-looking and well liked by his peers and suppliers, was somewhat different from the other Young Turks. Frank, as senior vice-president and general merchandise manager of all apparel in Macy's New York, the premier job in what had to be the most profitable end of the business, had intelligence and sensitivity. But when

Doroff's merchandise divisions floundered—Finkelstein was an avid student of every possible measure of the store's performance—he called Frank in and discussed the problem with him. He told Doroff that he had to be tougher with the vendors, that, in effect, he had to be a "killer."

Finally, in 1983, he reluctantly called in Frank and told him that he would probably do better elsewhere and should seek another job. Frank discussed the situation with Ben Doroff, his father and himself a highly talented merchant as the executive vice-president for sales promotion at John Wanamaker. Ben agreed that Frank may not have the right chemistry for Finkelstein but could probably find a more compatible job in another retail chain. Early that year, Frank Doroff moved to Federated Department Stores in a post at Bullock's, the Los Angeles division, where he eventually did very well, finally becoming its president.

Frank's relatively easy move to another major retailer, as well as the knowledge that other Macy executives were more readily accepting calls from executive recruiters seeking to place them in other jobs, must have been annoying to Finkelstein. With Macy's stunning turn-around of recent years, it seemed that everyone was eager to cherry-pick among his executives, siphoning off untold time and expenditures given by Macy to train its most promising people. The business, Ed realized, was becoming more avaricious, more carnivorous in grabbing talent away from companies that had nurtured it.

With Brown and others, he began working on a method to stem the exodus by granting executives "balloon payments," in which desirable people would be offered special bonuses each year to stay on but collectible only at the end of a third year.

But he knew that the balance of money and motivation against the pressures he had to exert would be tenuous. Salaries, bonuses, and deferred comp would not be enough compared with some manner of entrepreneurial involvement.

The difficulties of managing that balance, the problems of Macy's dramatic profit decline, and the concern over a possible hostile take-over weighed on Finkelstein throughout 1983, 1984, and into 1985. It was an odd commentary on corporate success that success itself wasn't sufficient. You had to shore up your defenses, always guard your flanks because the attack could come from various directions and in other different forms. What could one do?

*　　*　　*

And there stood the leveraged buyout. It beckoned to him more and more, holding promises and incentives that little else seemed to offer. He had to convince the directors that it was the best, the only, thing that Macy's could do, for its own good. And that took some doing.

Between the June 25, 1985, board meeting when Finkelstein had first announced his management buyout proposal and the final meeting on October 21 of the same year, there were ten meetings of the board of directors, as well as several of a special committee of eleven nonmanagement directors of the total board of seventeen to study the proposal and alternatives. During that time, the outside directors had wavered from a staunch opposition to his proposal to giving in on the condition that it be on a basis of at least $70 a share. What had prompted the outside directors to fall into line? On the other hand, why shouldn't they, when Macy's stock had risen on October 17 to $47.125, a good increase for the period but much under the $70 level offered? But why had they cautioned Finkelstein at the first meeting to withdraw his request to make a buyout presentation? Was it that they were dismayed by the idea of a board chairman donning another hat to buy a company that was already paying him $781,000? Or that they wanted more time to consider it? Finkelstein had agreed, saying he would put his idea "on hold" and not contact any financing sources about a buyout, but he reserved the right to present it for later consideration.

On July 1, the nonmanagement directors met with Finkelstein and Handler, Goldman Sachs, the financial adviser, and Ira Millstein, counsel to the Macy chief, to discuss the buyout idea and its rationale. At the initial board meeting, Finkelstein explained that Macy had recently been experiencing difficulties retaining "key middle-management" personnel, that a broadly based management-directed buyout would be the most effective means of addressing this management stability issue and motivating managers to keep Macy an exciting and innovative merchandiser. And, then, said a May 23, 1986, proxy, "Mr. Finkelstein noted he believed Macy was likely to be entering a period in which growth in sales and earnings would be slower than that experienced in recent years and that, during this period, the appreciation in the market value of the Common Shares, on which much of Macy's existing incentive compensation program is based, might not be as favorable as it had been in recent years."

But only three or four senior executives had actually departed. If many had, and money was the primary lure, the rationale would have meant something. And what of Finkelstein's own querulous comment to his closest associates that he himself was "getting on to sixty without an awful lot to show for it"? And, then again, if Macy's stock wasn't going to perform well, what about the non-Macy shareholders? What did they deserve?

At a board meeting on July 10, 1985, Finkelstein suggested that Lawrence E. Fouraker, a nonmanagement director, a fellow of the John F. Kennedy School of Government at Harvard University and a former dean of faculty at the Harvard Business School, organize a special committee of nonmanagement directors to review the issues raised by the buyout. He did.

On July 22, Finkelstein, Handler, and their colleagues laid out the management stability problem and stressed that the future stability of Macy's middle management was a matter of serious concern to them. And at a July 23 directors' meeting, all the nonmanagement directors were appointed to the special committee, headed by Harold Shaub, retired president and chief executive officer of Campbell Soup Company. The committee also included two former Macyites. They were Kenneth Straus, the son of Jack Straus and the former chairman of the R. H. Macy Corporate Buying division, who had retired from Macy in February 1985 at age fifty-nine, and Donald B. Smiley, the former Macy chairman and chief executive, who had retired in July 1980 at sixty-five. Interestingly enough, according to the proxy statement for the November 26 annual meeting, they were as of September 25, 1985, the first and third largest shareholders, respectively, of Macy, with Ed Finkelstein the second largest. That meant that when the full board finally approved in principle a buyout at $70 a share, both outside directors made a profit in the millions of dollars. Ken Straus had 719,219 shares and Smiley had 105,462 shares. Finkelstein had 143,460 and Mark Handler had 84,500. Should Straus and Smiley, with so much of an investment in Macy stock, been on the special committee formed to objectively weigh an internal buyout at more than a $20-a-share premium?

His colleagues knew that Ken Straus was unhappy about the executives' buyout, but when asked if he didn't want to comment, he replied to the effect that he "wouldn't dignify what Finkelstein did by engaging in a public debate." Smiley, too—along with Stephen M. DeBrul, Jr., another special committee member and a business consultant and private banker—was reported to be initially unhappy with the Finkelstein buyout proposals. But when invited to discuss the procedures of the board in terms of the buyout, Smiley refused, explaining, "I'll stand on the record." Unfortunately, the record, in terms of the two annual meetings and the various proxies relating to them, says very little about Smiley's conduct. As was charged at both the meetings when shareholders voted on the buyout, they had little information compared with what the directors had, yet were asked to vote on an issue that was important to all of them.

Before the July 23 meeting ended, Finkelstein said he hoped that by the end of September the board would be able to decide either to allow him to pursue the buyout or to "pursue other alternatives." A merger with Associated Dry Goods, Dayton Hudson, even, perhaps, Federated? Or a better job for himself and his cohorts?

In August 1985, in a series of meetings with a working unit of the special committee, such issues as the buyout, management stability, and ways of addressing the latter continued to be discussed. On August 29, the special committee also retained its own special legal counsel.

September arrived and to Finkelstein's dismay the special committee still seemed undecided. Was an impasse building between the management and the nonmanagement directors? Within a few days, Finkelstein took matters in hand and on September 9 delivered a letter to Harold Shaub, the special committee chairman. The management letter, signed by Finkelstein, Handler, Herb Friedman, Bobby Friedman, Art Reiner, and James O. York, president of R. H. Macy Properties Division, was astonishing in its presumption. It asserted that each signee had concluded that as a director, his fiduciary obligations to the shareholders would compel him "to vote to encourage the management directors to proceed with an offer for presentation to the Board." The logic was purportedly altruistic. They said that the buyout was financially feasible at the time but that the circumstances that made it so might not continue.

Further, they said that should a management group ultimately offer Macy's shareholders an all-cash transaction involving a significant premium over the then current market prices, it was likely, "given the then current attitude of shareholders and the makeup of Macy's shareholders," that the offer would be "most favorably received and would be approved by Macy's shareholders." What was more, the management directors believed that their fiduciary responsibilities mandated that a director must have "serious and substantial reasons to impede the shareholders from receiving an all-cash offer which the management directors believed would exceed the present value of Macy's

future growth and which the management directors believed the
shareholders almost certainly would accept from a group with a demonstrated ability to run Macy properly."

The signers added that the proposal that they were contemplating
was, in their view as directors, clearly in the best interests of the
shareholders, Macy's other constituencies, and, thus, Macy. In their
view, the common share purchase price "would be attractive to shareholders, management would be motivated by equity ownership, and a
highly motivated management would produce beneficial results to
Macy's customers, suppliers, and communities."

This communication speeded the process of decision. Within a
week, a dizzy schedule of meetings brought matters to a head—and an
unpleasant one for the Finkelstein team. On September 12, the special committee met to review all that had happened since it had been
set up on July 23 and to discuss the September 9 letter. The committee
decided to retain a financial adviser to assist it and to meet again
September 18. On September 13, it retained James D. Wolfensohn, a
well-regarded investment banker, to act as its financial adviser.

On September 17, having no reply from the special committee, the
management directors acted again. They delivered a letter advising
the committee that they had determined to proceed with a buyout
proposal in which Macy's shareholders would receive $68 a common
share. The special committee didn't buy it. The next day, the nonmanagement directors unanimously adopted a resolution to be presented to the full board the same day stating that it was inappropriate
and not in the best interests of Macy for the management directors to
seek to purchase Macy "by procedures initiated and directed by them
and that, accordingly, the management directors were directed not to
proceed at that time with the preparation of a proposal. And in the light
of recent discussions concerning the maximization of shareholder
values, the Special Committee was instructed to consider all appropriate ways of maximizing shareholder values, including the possibility of
a buyout of Macy" as the management directors had proposed. The
committee was also authorized to engage such independent advisers as
it deemed appropriate to confer with Macy management and other
appropriate parties "and to report its findings to the Board on an
expeditious basis. Macy's officers and employees were requested to
cooperate fully with the Special Committee." The same day, Shaub
presented the committee's recommendations to the board and a vote
was taken. All eleven nonmanagement directors voted for it; the six
management directors voted against. The resolution passed.

Finkelstein took it stoically, according to close associates, but inside, he must have been crushed. He told his people that their only hope was that Wolfensohn would be unable to find a third party willing to pay a 50 percent premium over the market price for Macy's. (Later, the investment banker contacted "numerous third parties" to obtain an offer to acquire Macy on terms more favorable to Macy's shareholders than those offered by the management team. Five requested and received copies of a confidential memorandum pertaining to Macy; two met with Finkelstein and Handler in early December 1985 but neither made any offer.)

In the meantime, on October 16 and 18, the special committee met with its legal counsel and Wolfensohn to consider various alternatives. Wolfensohn was instructed to meet with Goldman Sachs, financial adviser to the management group, study the feasibility of its buyout offer in "the light of then current circumstances and market conditions," and report to the committee as soon as possible. On October 17, Macy's stock rose to $47.125, up $2.375 a share. Not a word about the buyout offer had appeared in the media or on the financial tape, but it seems apparent, with a gain of that dimension in one day, that the news was getting to the street and profits were being made.

On October 18, "certain members" of the special committee met with Finkelstein and Handler and told them that the management directors could make their proposal. It was an oblique approval. According to the May 23, 1985, proxy statement:

> At this meeting, Mr. Finkelstein and Mr. Handler were advised that, while the Special Committee did not wish to initiate a sale of Macy, either to a group led by the management directors or to a third party, and was not prepared to encourage Mr. Finkelstein to proceed to prepare a buyout proposal, it was willing to permit the management directors to proceed with the preparation of a buyout proposal so long as the management directors agreed to proceed subject to certain conditions, including the condition that any proposal be at a price of $70 per Common Share in cash. The Special Committee members also stated that if the management directors proceeded to prepare a buyout proposal, the Special Committee would also seek and consider proposals for the acquisition of Macy from third parties. Mr. Finkelstein and Mr. Handler agreed to abide by such conditions.

Three days later, on October 21, the special committee unanimously endorsed the management group's request to submit its proposal. But some other conditions were added, according to the proxy statement. In addition to the stricture that the management offer be at least for $70 per share in cash, the committee's resolution directed that

(i) any management proposal should be submitted to the Board by December 1, 1985, and would be required to remain open for 45 days, (ii) any management proposal must contain a detailed financing plan for both the debt and equity portions of the financing therefore and be accompanied by a letter from Goldman Sachs to the effect that they are highly confident that such financing could be arranged and by acceptable proposal letters from lead financing sources, (iii) if the management directors proceeded with the preparation of a proposal, the Special Committee would seek and consider proposals for the acquisition of Macy from third parties, (iv) any merger agreement ultimately entered into with the management directors would not contain any "lockup" or "crown jewel" options relating to Macy's equity securities or its assets or business, (v) the management directors would be required to cooperate with bona fide prospective third-party bidders in providing information about Macy and (vi) should the Special Committee ultimately approve a bid from a third party, the management directors would be required to assist such third party during a reasonable transition period, should such management directors determine not to be employed by such third party.

That very same Monday, the committee resolution was unanimously approved by a unanimous vote of the full Macy board. And that afternoon Finkelstein and Handler issued a publicity release to the effect that management directors intended to make a buyout proposal at $70 a share in cash, a total of $3.6 billion. It would be the largest takeover of a retailer in history and the first leveraged buyout of a major retail chain.

The announcement produced a bombshell on Wall Street, sending Macy's stock up by $16.125 a share on October 22, 1985, to $63.25. The fact that that rise fell $6.75 a share short of the $70 offering price was seen on Wall Street as evidence that investors lacked confidence that the deal would go through. The reason for this was that the price was so high, so deliberately preemptive, that obtaining the right financing to support it would be a nearly impossible hurdle. The fact that later the bidders had to cut their offer to $68 a share in order to interest the lenders later confirmed this, and the $70 a share offer remained a stumbling block, not merely to financiers but to investors' confidence. Three weeks later, the Macy stock remained more than $5 a share below the glowing offering price.

Could Finkelstein, Handler, and their cohorts cope with interest and principal payments equal to or greater than their annual profits? That question was at the core of the doubt. It would be one thing to mount a leveraged buyout. It would be another to pay for it at a difficult time; a third to still make a profit; and a fourth—the most important of all—to make it work.

Later, Finkelstein told me of some of his conflicts about the decision he had to make.

"I saw things happening in the retail business that could affect us. I knew that Tom Macioce, the chairman of Allied Stores, a couple of years ago was trying to put together an LBO but couldn't because Allied's earnings weren't strong enough. Then Bill Arnold, the chairman of Associated Dry Goods and I met and we went out to my terrace because sound in my office carries out to the hall. And we agreed to merge Associated and Macy, with our company paying about $1.8 billion for ADG. He was very sick, as everyone knew, and he wanted to assure the continuance of the company. I offered to make him co–chief executive, but on the way down in the elevator he changed his mind. Later, David Farrell, the chairman of the May Department Stores Company, began trying to buy Associated. It was apparent to me that any undervalued company—most big retailers are undervalued—was open game for any company with money.

"In my mind, I went through all the possibilities—buying back Macy stock, leaving my job and making a bid for the company from the outside, and so on. But none of these seemed to do what I wanted. I decided to do the toughest thing of all, a leveraged buyout." It would be the toughest, he implied, because he would be investing his own money and that of his colleagues and risking it all.

"Why? We were losing people. We were too short-term oriented. A month, two, or even a quarter doesn't matter much in our type of business. It takes a couple of years. I knew, too, that our down year of 1985 had to be improved and we could only do it by concentrating on our business, offering incentive to our best people so that they could work harder. We found that an executive who put in, say, $70,000— which he could get by cashing in his Macy stock and rolling it over to pay his share—could, if our calculations were right, build it into $3.5 million to $4 million if he worked hard and could wait it out. And we figured that we could get about 350 people into it, top executives, senior vice-presidents, and so on. And we could create some dilution so that more lower-rank executives could get involved. For $17,500, they could get as much as $1.5 million.

"We not only had a good record of earnings," Finkelstein continued, "but the combination of our depreciation of things we had installed in earlier years and our cash flow made us a good candidate for an LBO. It would mean some high debt and hard work but we were convinced it was the only way for us to go.

"When I told Jack Straus, he wasn't happy about it. He had been out of the business really for a decade and when he was here he only had about $1 million or so in Macy stock. It was then $10 a share. Later, when it climbed to $50 a share, his holdings were worth $50 million. He had nothing to complain about. The Straus family wouldn't be happy about it, either. But altogether they owned about 1.5 percent of the stock. Our LBO group held about 1 percent. It wasn't like the Haas family that owned Levi Strauss when Bob Haas presented as *fait accompli* his offer to his board. He and his family owned about 35 percent of the business. But I thought Jack Straus's response was ungenerous, ungentlemanly.

"As for the shareholders," he said, "they would get the offer at a premium, $70 a share, if that's what it would be, against the current market price of about only $46 a share. Our bid was to be preemptive. There were rumors that other companies were interested in Macy but nothing seemed to be happening."

In one sense, the Straus family had bowed out of Macy ownership long ago. When the Strauses had floated their first public issue in 1924, it was with the tacit understanding among the older and younger members that they would gradually reduce their holdings over the ensuing decades so as to both diversify their investments and to allow the public to increase its ownership. From a 100 percent interest in the twenties, the Strauses cut their interest to about 20 percent by the mid-sixties through additional stock issues or private sales and to about 2 percent by the mid-eighties.

So on Monday, October 21, Finkelstein, Handler, and other senior members of Macy management made their announcement. After sixty-three years of public ownership, Macy's would buy all its stock and go private again.

PUSHING THE
GAME PLAN UPHILL

In the fall of 1987, a rumor spread through the Macy community. Competitors and executive recruiters heard it; the press picked up its ears; Macyites started a guessing game. As suspicious glances met questioning eyes, uncertainty grew in Macy's new, private world.

The rumor was that one of the top officers was about to defect, pull away from the buyout and perhaps go to the competition. He, or she, had had enough. The rumor, feeding on itself, quickly centered on a divisional president, maybe even a chairman. Could it be Arthur Reiner, chief of the New York division? Bobby Friedman, head of Bamberger's? Terry Motoris, the company's highest-ranking woman, who had succeeded Leslie Ball as Atlanta president? No, not Terry, whose continued promotions defied reports of Finkelstein's chauvinism. Or, possibly, Herb Yalof, the New York president under Reiner, who had already departed once, resigning in 1976 as Bam's senior vice-president to join Associated Dry Goods' Hahne division in New Jersey as president, only to return in two and a half years to Macy.

There was already ample precedent for defection among the loyal ranks.

The most notable was that of Matt Langweber, who was clearly marked for great things at Macy's. Rather tall but stocky, handsome and outgoing, with closely-cropped brown hair and a confident manner, he had an executive salesman's manner about him. In a decade, he had advanced from Bamberger's training squad to senior vice-president in charge of several women's apparel divisions at Bamberger's. Everyone at the top liked his drive, his youthful enthusiasm, and especially his ability to put together creative combinations of concepts and suppliers. At 35, he appeared to be a potential executive vice-president and ultimately a divisional president; he was naturally included in the buyout group. Yet on a Monday morning in April 1986, he sat in the office of Bobby Friedman, Bam's chairman, and said, "Bobby, I'm resigning."

Friedman stiffened. "You're what?"

"I'm quitting."

"Why? What are you gonna do?"

"I'm going into business for myself. I'm joining Phil Schlein's U.S. Venture Partners and starting a little retail chain of my own."

Bobby had paled. "Schlein! My God. Is there anything we can do to make you stay?" he demanded.

Matt shook his head. Bobby regarded him with shock and dismay. The buyout was directly aimed at keeping such productive and promising young executives as Langweber within the fold; they were the bone marrow of Macy's turnaround and the hope of its future. Friedman was about to convene his weekly executive committee meeting and Matt had to attend so as not to indicate that something was amiss. But after a few minutes, Friedman abruptly adjourned the meeting. Privately, he told Matt not to return when it resumed later but to go to his office and wait for Friedman's summons. Matt understood: Bobby had a big chore; he had to tell Finkelstein.

Returning to his office, Langweber was glad that he would not have to face the Macy chief, whom he didn't doubt would be rough on Friedman. His knees felt weak and he sat down to wait, feeling the tug of mixed emotions. He had truly enjoyed his Bam's experience and yet he felt himself still only a cog in a big wheel which could eventually grind him up.

But Mother Macy had been good to him. Matt, born in Queens, New York, had graduated with finance and business degrees from Lehigh University and the Columbia University Graduate School of Business, and had joined Bam's training squad in 1976, drawn by the division's big expansion drive. Two months later, he was an assistant buyer. Thereafter, at least once a year he received a promotion, so that by August 1981, five years after joining, he had been appointed a vice-president and merchandise administrator of two women's apparel departments. He seemed to take easily and with enjoyment to each new responsibility, and they continued to be handed to him. In 1983, he was put in charge of Bam's Northern New Jersey stores as group vice-president, and in January 1984, he became senior vice-president for misses' sportswear, lingerie, dresses, and junior sportswear.

"I was pleased with my advancement overall, but I honestly think I deserved it," Langweber told me. "I consistently delivered the business, the profits. Mark Handler, who preceded Bobby Friedman as Bam's big boss, always encouraged executives to reach out and I was an apt pupil. Mark's idea was to take a sportswear division and split it into four departments. This gave each a big shot so that the total had more potential. It was a very go-go attitude. And I went with it."

As a merchandise administrator, he decided that he wanted to apply the "reaching out" principle to the Liz Claiborne line. "We were already doing a lot with Liz," he said. "There were a lot of sportswear houses, but I liked the freshness of her designs combined with the good taste of her fabrics. So in 1981 I told Bam's executive committee that I wanted to step out in all the stores with special sections of Liz. I knew that I was asking a lot. Every inch counted in the stores, each was expected to pull good business. The stores, too, were huge palaces where one particular section could get lost. But they agreed and I got it going.

"Within a short time, we were doing a ton of business with Liz," Langweber said. "Our computer report showed that our rates of sale were wonderful and always growing. Everyone was delighted. It was one of those fortunate, synergistic things."

After being promoted for that coup, Matt found himself in charge of menswear where business was difficult—men weren't anxious in 1980 to become peacocks. The Christmas season was imminent and something was needed to energize sales. Knowing that Bam's would be reluctant to expend more funds on a static department, Matt proposed that the chain issue a special supplement on menswear. He told Roger Markfield, senior vice-president for menswear, "I know that we don't normally do much sales promotion on menswear. But I think the timing is right, with the holiday coming up and there's all that pent-up demand among men for clothes and sportswear. Why don't we take a shot at it?"

It was daring in another way. Supplements, used jointly in newspapers and in-store booklets or sent to homes, were usually devoted to home furnishings, on the basis that such purchases needed some reflection by consumers and were usually retained at least several days in the home. The booklet would cost Bam's about $200,000. "How many suppliers would kick in with cooperative advertising money?" Matt asked. "I guess it was one of those cases where I wasn't smart enough to know it couldn't be done. Markfield agreed to do it and we got a lot of support from the suppliers. And we put the whole darned thing together in four weeks, a record time. It clicked, and very well, too. So well that it became an annual thing at Bam's."

As he continued to wait for Bobby's call, Matt recalled the excitement and concern that he had felt when he joined the buyout. "I was impressed by the projection that our investment could be mutliplied between twenty and fifty times if we could deliver and go public again." Yet, he said, the amount he invested was important to his wife and their two children. And it would mean working harder than ever over the next five years—the important ones between 35 and 40—for something that might or might not develop. "And, at the same time, there were other opportunities in retailing. One that especially intrigued me were specialty shops for the petite woman, who had been pretty much overlooked by the big stores," he said.

When Friedman finally summoned him, Matt found Bobby even paler and more shaken than before. In effect, Bobby was responsible for bringing Matt into the buyout group, so he was caught between Matt's defection and Finkelstein's great belief in personal loyalty.

His thin face tight with resentment, Bobby said, "I only hope that someday somebody does to you what you did to me today." After a pause, he added, "I want you to clear out of here as soon as you can."

In his office, Matt was surprised to find John Hegan, Bam's director of security, waiting for him. "Don't take any company papers with you," Hegan said, with a sheepish smile. "I was told to tell you that."

"I know, John, you're just doing your job," Matt said.

His phone rang. It was one of his merchandise administrators. "Matt, do you know that there's a security guy waiting outside your door," the young man said, "and there are two of them out on the lot checking your car?"

That afternoon, when he was ready to leave, Matt was called to the office of Rudy Borneo, Bam's president, where he found both Borneo and Shelly Bleiweiss, the division's personnel chief. They read him a legal statement. It said that since he had an "implied conflict," he was not to take any proprietary information with him or influence any other of Bam's personnel to leave with him. But Mike Balmuth, his top assistant, had also tendered his resignation to join Matt in the same venture, and they knew it.

"What's the problem?" Matt asked. "Other guys have left. And you can call off the security staff. Here are all my keys, and you can check the car if you want to."

Outside the office, he gave Borneo's secretary his "Q" book, which contained pertinent data on all his divisions. In the parking lot, he saw the guards by his car, one of whom handed him his keys. But angry and not wanting to show it, he instead walked across the street to a bar which Bam's people frequented. The word went out that he was there and soon half a dozen of his closest co-workers joined him. However, they didn't linger long.

It wasn't quite over. Two weeks later, a large contingent of Bam's executives and other employees arranged to give Langweber and Balmuth a farewell party at the Rusty Scupper, a West Orange, New Jersey, restaurant. "Come wish the boys the best of luck!" the invitation read. When Ed Finkelstein heard about the party, he phoned one of the administrators involved and warned that under no circumstances could the party be held. It wasn't.

"I feel pretty bad about how it worked out," Langweber said. "I really loved working at Bam's. But it was the Schlein connection and the buyout that made Macy's so upset at me. My leaving was a slap in the face to the buyout. I really didn't mean to rain on Ed's parade, but I guess I did."

In a few weeks, however, the rumor of a top-level defector died. The Macy entrepreneurs breathed a sigh of relief. If one top-tier member pulled away, others might, too, and the whole fabric might just come apart. And so the mood among the 350—and the 350 under them and the hundreds under them—swung back to its normal two poles.

Agony and joy, joy and agony; through all of 1986 and most of 1987, the emotions shifted. Among the Finkelstein team and the premier 350, there was the joy of budding achievement, of a sure inching toward goals, and hope and then confidence that they could even beat the schedule. But there was agony, too. All were working harder, putting in more time and ignoring their families more than ever for the lure of wealth. And it would be at least four years, perhaps five, before Macy could go public again and everyone could cash in.

And among the many executives who had not been chosen for the buyout team, there was emptiness and frustration. A cap had been screwed on their careers, it seemed, as the static roles of the buyout group kept the others down. Why hadn't they been chosen, they wondered; what incentives did they have? The slow exodus continued. Token incentives from the Finkelstein team were meaningless, compared with their frustration at not being anointed, not being given equal opportunity.

At the pinnacle, too, the joy was mixed with agony. Finkelstein, who had gone through the wringer first in convincing his board to go along with the buyout and then in obtaining financing for it, found himself bouncing from a sense of achievement to one of frustration and back again. Others in the buying group and those who opposed them also felt something of that emotional push and pull. Attitudes, of course, were still hot on both sides, and so the proxy statements and the prospectuses that recounted the buyout's trials and tribulations were reviewed over and over again by supporters and critics alike. And new interpretations, based on individual predilections, were put on them.

If financing was the real binder—and it was—had they put the deal together with glue or a Band-Aid? Was the package sound enough to bear pressure and risk?

The Macy executives would kick in a total of slightly more than $17 million to buy 20 percent of a company for $3.6 billion. But who would foot the rest? Goldman Sachs had scoured the country and abroad to find the amenable lenders. Meanwhile, Finkelstein was pleased to receive calls from others interested in participating in the equity or to have them return calls that he had made. As the financing quest continued, an interesting complement of equity investors enlisted.

Laurence A. Tisch, the new chief executive officer of Columbia Broadcasting System and chairman of Loew's Corporation, convinced Loew's to become a 14.9 percent investor by acquiring 1.12 million preferred shares of the Macy Acquiring Corporation, as the management buyout vehicle was named. A. Alfred Taubman, the prominent shopping center developer, chairman of Taubman Holdings, took 5 percent of the preferred. Henry A. Kissinger, the former secretary of state and chairman of his consulting company, bought 6.03 percent. All three investors were named to the new Macy board of directors.

All the preferred shares brought a kitty of $282.5 million, covering the majority of the equity portion of the $3.6 billion financing. Biggest investor in the equity was the General Electric Credit Corporation, which became a 24.9 percent equity owner with its purchase of 1.9 million shares. Mutual Shares Corporation, which operates mutual funds, bought 942,988 shares and Michael A. Price, its chief, purchased 28,628 shares, the total giving them a combined 12.96 percent share in the preferred. Goldman Sachs bought 189,298 shares, its limited partnerships took another 18,930 shares, and Sidney J. Weinberg, Jr., a partner in Goldman Sachs, personally bought 12,620 shares, or a total of about 3 percent. Price, Weinberg, and Dan L. Hale, senior vice-president of General Electric Credit, were also appointed to the new board.

What of the Macy buyout group? With outside investors taking the preferred stock or 81 percent of the total equity, the Macy management group received 18 percent of the equity in the form of slightly more than 1 million common shares for about $17 million. Ed Finkelstein, who had owned 143,460 common shares of the old Macy Corporation, received 437,500 common shares, or 25 percent, of the new Macy. Mark Handler, who owned 84,500 old Macy shares, got 218,750 shares, or 12.5 percent, of the total. Art Reiner converted his 65,356 shares to 87,500 new shares, or 5 percent. Bobby Friedman, 53,110, got 70,000 shares, or 4 percent. Herb Friedman, 46,400, got 17,500 shares, or 1 percent. (He was sixty-two, two years older than Finkelstein and already looking to retirement three years hence.) Hal Kahn, with an unspecified amount of old shares, received 52,500 new ones, or 3 percent.

The new Macy was lucrative for the buying group in more than just the conversion privileges. In that first year of the buyout, Finkelstein's salary was raised from his $780,696 with deferred compensation of $150,000 to $1,205,000. Handler, with a salary of $574,000 and deferred comp of $140,000, was boosted to $877,338. Both then signed five-year contracts—Finkelstein at $1,050,000 a year and Handler at $800,000 a year—and both agreed to stay on in their respective posts for at least five years to satisfy the conditions of the financing.

And it wasn't merely money and ownership that Finkelstein obtained for his efforts to put together a buying team. The management investors signed a voting trust agreement providing that Finkelstein would be the sole voting trustee on all matters on which the management shareholders were entitled to vote. This gave him great power, not only to keep the others in line but to designate who would be on the new board. The agreement called for him to name the majority of the board, while the nonmanagement investors designating directors had to be sure that they were "reasonably satisfactory" to Finkelstein as the "management trustee." If for some reason Finkelstein was unable to serve in that capacity, Handler was to be his successor.

The total financing, a whopping $3.7 billion, was needed for the following: $3.5 billion to buy 51,489,632 common shares at $68 per share; $24 million for the Macy stock option cash-out, or 655,580 shares at $68 each less a weighted average exercise price of $31.41 a share; $17 million for the redemption of preferred shares and $165 million for transaction fees from banks, investment bankers, and attorneys.

There were eleven sources to be tapped for the total financing, ranging from $800 million for senior real estate debt to $17 million in revenues from the sale of 1,750,000 shares of the acquiring company's common stock at $10 a share. There were $735 million in bank loans for one-year and six-year terms, there were four classes of notes or debentures providing a total of $1.6 billion, and there was the acquiring company's preferred stock with a value of $283 million. The Macy Revolving Credit Facility, the company's finance subsidiary, would provide $178 million, and excess cash in Macy was worth $94 million.

In other words, the leveraged buyout was to be consummated by use of Macy real estate, its ability to draw loans, offer notes and debentures, issue both preferred and common stock, and, in the bargain, use $94 million of cash in the Macy till. With those total funds, the Macy management team was legally able to buy operating control of a company that had first belonged to Rowland H. Macy, then to the Straus family, and then for six decades to thousands of public shareholders.

Security pledged to the lending agencies showed how valuable they regarded Macy's assets and how the acquirers were able to purchase the company they worked for by applying the property and values built up by it over a period of decades. Citibank, Manufacturers Hanover Trust Company, and Bankers Trust Company, three of New York's largest banking institutions, agreed to provide about $861 million of the total bank loans. The same banks, acting as agents, were also able to obtain commitments from several other banks to constitute a syndicate covering almost $1.2 billion of the total bank loans. These included a one-year term loan, a six-year term loan, and the Macy Revolving Credit Facility. The one-year loan was secured by Macy's and its affiliates' interest in ten shopping centers, wholly or partly owned. The six-year loan and the revolving credit facility were secured by a group of collateral properties, pledges, and liens, including all the capital stock of Macy's and its affiliates; liens on notes receivable from the sale of stores; accounts owing from the American Express Company; other accounts receivables; certain tangible personal property other than inventory and general intangibles, including trade names and trademarks; junior liens on seventy-five stores; and liens on substantially all of Macy's other property and interests in real property.

What about repayment of the loans? The $225 million one-year loan, of course, was to be paid in a year. The six-year loan called for repayment of installments from $5 million to $95 million in six-month increments, concluding with a $30 million payment in June 1992. The bank syndicate was much impressed with Macy's shopping center holdings, and as it turned out negotiations were apparently already under way to sell them. But in the May 1986 proxy statement for the special November stockholders' meeting that overwhelmingly approved the leveraged buyout, the bank deal provided that any sale of the centers would go first to satisfy in full the one-year loan and the overage would pay for as much of the six-year loan as possible. The banks had received appraisals that the shopping centers had a "fair market" value of at least $300 million. In early November, the Macy Acquiring Corporation and Westfield Holdings Ltd., of Sydney, Australia, jointly announced that three Macy centers and a forty-four-acre development tract in Paramus, New Jersey, had been acquired by Westfield for $363.5 million. Thus, the first-year loan was quickly paid by the sale of the Garden State Plaza in Paramus, the South Shore Mall in Bay Shore, New York, the Bay Fair Mall in San Francisco, and the tract adjacent to the Garden State Plaza in Paramus. After selling these properties, Macy continued to operate its stores there under a long-term lease with Westfield. Discussions were also under way by Macy to sell its interests in four other shopping centers to several parties.

It was obvious that Macy's management was able to consummate its buyout in a substantial way because of the value of the company's real assets. The seventy-five store properties used as collateral for the bank loans and the credit facility were appraised by the banks at not less than $1.4 billion. No one, it appeared, was taking any chances on questionable values. Between the shopping centers and the seventy-five store properties, the appraised value equaled more than 45 percent of the total indebtedness.

General Electric Credit agreed to purchase for $459.6 million a combination of $400 million in senior subordinated debentures and shares of Macy Acquiring Corporation preferred stock in an amount convertible into 20 percent of the company's common stock after the merger. GEC bought the debentures with the same conditions or collateral with which the banks granted their loans. But the banks had the right to approve the exercise of those conditions by GEC, and because of the purchase of the debentures, Macy had to furnish registration statements to the Securities and Exchange Commission.

Prudential Life Insurance Company committed itself to a loan of $800 million secured by first or second participating mortgages on seventy-one Macy stores and fixed rate mortgages on the other four stores. Besides the basic 12 percent rate of interest, a cap of 13 percent interest allowed Prudential additional return. At maturity of the fifteen-year loans, Prudential would receive added interest if the real estate value of the properties increased (Macy's Herald Square store was a significant element in the loan security). And if the loans were repaid before maturity, there was to be a "substantial prepayment penalty." In all, it was a sweet deal for Prudential.

The return for its troubles was a very healthy 28 percent, according to Prudential sources. What follows is a conversation with a Prudential official, who asked not to be identified because it would cause him embarrassment within the company. The discussion was held in July 1987, a year after the Macy buyout.

"We have about $800 million of mortgages with Macy properties," he said, "so that I have been a very close observer of what's going on there. Macy's is holding its own, not quite up to the projections which they give us at Prudential. We made a hell of a deal on those Macy properties where we get a return of almost 28 percent."

"You mean as part of the LBO?"

"Yes. We cherry-picked the stores that we took mortgages on. That was number one. And then we negotiated an override on the sales at those stores, not the profits. It was all in all a much better deal than we usually get. And that was because we knew that they would push like hell for volume, and in pushing like hell for volume it ultimately has to be at the expense of profit. So we based the override on sales."

"So the pressure is on to build volume?"

"Right. You see more and more evidence of it in different ways. Like a tremendous unhappiness developing in the cadre of 350 participants in the purchase. They're working seven days a week, twelve hours a day. They are being pushed like crazy—"

"The participants tell you and the Prudential people this?"

"Yes, and others we know. I've not only heard it from the people themselves, but in a few instances from the parents of the younger people in the group who are very concerned about the way they are being pushed."

"Does that mean there's a failure of confidence in the payoff?"

"There's getting to be considerable apprehension, because there's an awareness that with the slightest glitch—like June wasn't a very good month in the retail business—the plan can go haywire and there's just so much demand that can be put on the vendors with slower pay and with concessions by the vendor on advertising. The vendors, too, are feeling the pressure from Macy," he said.

The buyout group's anxiety to put the deal together also led to a binge of expenses paid for the transaction. The estimated expenses and fees caused by the Macy management buyout, totalling $165 million, broke down as follows:

Goldman Sachs	$ 30,250,000
Shearson Lehman Brothers	4,750,000
James D. Wolfensohn	5,500,000
Bank fees and non-bank financing costs	75,700,000
Legal fees	10,710,000
Accounting fees	1,750,000
Appraisal fees	540,000
Proxy solicitation fees	17,500
S.E.C. fees	708,400
N.A.S.D. fees	5,100
Trustees' fees	208,600
Printing and mailing	1,000,000
Redemption and paying agents' fees and costs	15,000
Transfer agent fees	21,000
Accelerated payments in connection with deferred compensation payments	10,000,000
Miscellaneous	23,800,000
Total	$164,975,600

Of the total, about $51.8 million would have to be paid whether or not the buyout materialized. Goldman Sachs was in for more than the itemized list indicated, with its fees to amount to a dazzling $35 million. If the merger were abandoned, Goldman Sachs could still walk away with a cool $20 million. But the investment banking house had to buy its way in, too, purchasing about $7.5 million of the new Macy's preferred shares.

There were many other costs, all, of course, paid directly or indirectly by the very shareholders of the old Macy's so that the new Macy's could be established. Not that they were asked to approve those expenses; that is not the way standard corporate democracy works. In November 1985, after the board and the shareholders had approved the buyout, the directors authorized a special payment or supplemental compensation of $600,000 to the members of the special committee "in recognition of the time and effort previously devoted and to be devoted to Macy's affairs in connection with the Special Committee's responsibilities."

Harold Shaub, the committee chairman, received $150,000. Awards of $75,000 were given to Barbara Scott Preiskel, an attorney; Stephen M. DeBrul, Jr., the banker and consultant; Robert G. Schwartz, chairman of Metropolitan Life Insurance Company; and Donald B. Smiley, the former Macy chairman. The other six members of the special committee got $25,000 each.

How well did the committee and its special financial adviser, James Wolfensohn, the principal advisers to the Macy board, perform their duties? Their advice was crucial.

The full Macy board, noting that all its directors and all the officers intended to vote for the proposal of the management group, recommended to the shareholders of the old Macy that they vote for the proposal and approve the merger agreement. The board, in the May 1986 proxy statement, said that it considered the offer fair after considering that Wolfensohn deemed the consideration "fair" and that the special committee considered the terms of the merger "fair and in the best interests of the holders of Common Shares."

In its report rendered to the board, the special committee specified what it had considered. One item was that Wolfensohn said that the offer was fair. Another was its review of possible alternatives available to Macy, including the possible sale of Macy to a third party and continuing as an independent company. A third was the committee's knowledge of Macy's business, operations, properties, earnings, and prospects. Also examined were: certain information furnished the committee by management relative to Macy's future results and financial condition and forecasts; the committee's view of the going-concern value of Macy; the net book value of the common shares from time to time; the potential liquidation value of Macy; the provisions of the merger agreement with respect to the payment of additional dividends on the common shares; selected prices and premiums paid in recent acquisitions of retail companies; recent market prices for the common shares as well as market prices during the past several years and the relationship to the merger consideration; and the probable range of prices at which the common shares could be expected to trade under then current market conditions if the buyout proposal for $68 a share was not accepted "which the special committee believed would be lower than $68 a share."

Also considered by the committee was the fact that between October 21, 1985, and January 15, 1986, Wolfensohn at its direction had contacted, directly and indirectly, numerous third parties to obtain another offer to acquire Macy on terms better than the management proposal but that no such offer was received.

The group also took note of the value of Macy's assets, including its real estate and the book value per common share, which on November 2, 1985, and on February 1, 1986, was $26.03 and $27.82, respectively. "The Special Committee recognized that in connection with a liquidation of Macy many of its assets, particularly its inventories, would likely be sold only at substantial discounts from their book values. The Special Committee also recognized the substantial delays and uncertainties inherent in a liquidation of Macy. While the Special Committee recognized that the aggregate fair market value of Macy's assets, on a liquidation basis, might be more than the aggregate book value of such assets, the Special Committee concluded, after consulting with Wolfensohn, that the possible liquidation value per common share would likely be less than the $68 per share to be paid in the Merger," the committee's report read.

And, in a paragraph summing up the conflicting goals of old Macy shareholders and the management group and their equity investors, the committee report asserted

The Special Committee recognized that consummation of the Merger will deprive current holders of Common Shares (other than Acquiring Corp., its subsidiaries and those who will be security holders of Acquiring Corp.) of the opportunity to participate in any future growth of Macy and accordingly gave consideration to Macy's results of operations and Macy's future prospects in reaching its determination to recommend

approval and adoption of the Merger Agreement. The Special Committee was also aware that the Management Investors have a conflict of
interest in connection with the Merger because they will have a substantial equity investment in Acquiring Corp. and because certain Management Investors will be members of the management of Acquiring Corp.
or Macy, or both, after the Merger. Although the proposed high debt-to-
equity ratio of Macy after the Merger entails a risk to equity investors in
Acquiring Corp. and the resulting high debt service costs will adversely
affect earnings and the ability to pay dividends until such time as such
debt service costs are reduced, the Management Investors anticipate
that equity investments in Acquiring Corp. could substantially increase
in value as a result of a reduction over time in the indebtedness of Macy
incurred to finance the Merger.

So, one is tempted to ask, why were the old Macy shareholders not
given the same opportunity as the insiders? If the former would be
deprived of any opportunity to participate in Macy's future growth,
what is the value of having remained a loyal Macy shareholder for
decades? And if the latter were willing to put up their own funds
(almost exclusively Macy's stock options and employee stock purchases), why were the loyal, nonmanagement shareholders frozen out?
If one ever grows cynical over investing in American business, nothing
will provide more ammunition than the leveraged buyout or the cash
tender offer.

To be sure, the special committee also used an outside agency,
Valuation Research Corporation, to help determine the value of Macy's
business, its divisions, and subsidiaries in connection with the financing and to appraise certain Macy assets for tax and accounting purposes. A preliminary estimate was provided the committee and the full
board and their conclusion from it was that the merger terms were fair.

What of the composition of the special committee—was it objective
enough? The committee noted the following in the May 1986 proxy,
but it will scarcely ameliorate anyone's doubts: no committee member
was employed by Macy, the Acquiring Corporation, or any of their
affiliates. No member has or was expected to acquire any equity interest in the new Macy. But each committee member owned common
shares of the old Macy and Kenneth Straus owned preferred shares as
well. Barbara Preiskel and Lawrence Fouraker were directors of General Electric Company, the parent of the General Electric Credit
Corporation, and Fouraker was a director of Citibank. Both GECC and
Citibank "are expected to provide a portion of the Financing."

Added the committee report: "Members of the Special Committee have certain interests in the Merger that are in addition to the interests of the holders of Common Shares generally. These interests include the possible acceleration of certain deferred compensation payments and the possible modification of certain annuity arrangements with respect to certain of such persons and the payment of certain supplemental compensation and additional directors' retainer fees to all of such persons."

Was there, because of the possible conflicts of interest potentially residing in the special committee and among the management investors, any question of providing an ombudsman or special adviser for the old Macy shareholders? The old Macy board and the special committee responded to the question this way in the 1986 proxy:

> In view of the appointment of the Special Committee and the engagement of Wolfensohn and the special legal counsel by the Special Committee, and in view of the absence of any affiliation on the part of the members of the Special Committee with Acquiring Corp. or the Management Investors, neither the Board nor the Special Committee considered it necessary to retain an unaffiliated representative to act solely on behalf of the public shareholders of Macy for the purpose of negotiating the terms of the Merger or preparing a report concerning the fairness to such shareholders of the consideration to be received in the Merger.

So much for the special committee.

Wolfensohn, in his May 22, 1986, letter to the Macy board, noted that he had arrived at the "fair" conclusion based on a study of Macy financial reports, the company's current and historical financial position and operational results, a study of sundry matters as common share trading markets and available information of similar companies, discussions with Macy management personnel relative to their proposal, and the solicitation of acquisition proposals from other prospective purchasers. Wolfensohn did his job and decided that the management offer was fair; he received a fee of $5.5 million of what was still essentially the old shareholders' money.

As the new owners of Macy's assumed their new status and Macy became a private company, a rising chorus of questioning was heard amid some disenchantment with the whole concept of leveraged buyouts.

While leveraged buyouts represented only about 30 percent of some

three thousand business mergers in 1986, nonetheless, the LBO inci-
dence had grown since 1981 and the sharp rise in corporate debt was
beginning to arouse concern over undue financial leverage in American society. Congressional groups also expressed fears that too many
public shareholders were being deprived of profit that they would
have had if companies had remained public. The specific matter of the
LBO's "junk bonds," subordinated debt with a high yield not secured
against a company's assets but offered as stock options, was viewed as a
particular risk in a frisky investment market. Were the purveyors of
inside buyouts, the would-be entrepreneurs and the bankers who
craved the ever-growing fees, piling up so many billions of dollars of
debt that they were putting the U.S. economy at risk?

From 1985 through much of 1988, the big source of disenchantment
and doubt was whether the leveraged buyout was affecting adversely
companies whose managements, like Macy's, had generated an internal takeover. Many of those companies simply weren't making great
strides, either in terms of greater freedom and less external pressure
for the newly privatized companies or in successful operations without
dropping divisions and many jobs.

The private companies were finding that while they could effectively
put down class-action suits by annoyed public shareholders and avoid
the nitty-gritty scrutiny of Wall Street analysts, the equity investors
and bank lenders were tough critics, too. They wanted to know just
what was going on as often as they could and their pressure was an
unexpected burden on the managements who thought that life would
be calmer. Suppliers, who found themselves pushed to deliver
cheaper, better, and more profitable products so that debt could be
paid down, were irritated by such excessive demands. They were
skeptical, too, that the LBO-driven companies would succeed since
they were so laden with debt and didn't have the financial flexibility of
public companies.

From a performance standpoint, the results were very mixed.
Macy's had gone private to some extent because of fears that another
firm was stalking it. But others, such as Blue Bell Inc., the maker of
Wrangler jeans, in 1984 paid $144 million in "greenmail" to the Bass
family in Fort Worth, and then in November 1984 had mounted an
LBO when the Belzberg family of Canada, also active company
attackers, threatened a takeover. The company, fighting to reduce its
debt in a declining jeans market marked by heavy competition, was
able to increase the value of its assets by about 16 percent from

November 1984 through mid-1986. But its management team that had led the LBO realized an 800 percent rise in their investment by the time Blue Bell was sold in July of that year to VF Corporation for $800 million. VF, a leading apparel producer that already had the rival Lee brand of jeans, wanted the Wrangler brand to better compete with the leader, Levi Strauss. Bankers Trust, which held some of Blue Bell's senior loans, dreamed up the merger with VF and successfully proposed it to both sides.

It was even better for the Blue Bell management investors than going public because the merger was largely tax-free and didn't involve the risks of making an offering price to the public. The payoff was immediate, and the disparity between the company's growth and the huge individual payoff was no deterrent at all. For his $750,000 investment, Blue Bell chairman Edward J. Baumann received $6.2 million of VF stock. Four other officers and directors of Blue Bell, who had put in stakes of from $250,000 to $650,000, walked away with payouts of from $2.7 million to $3.2 million. How well had Blue Bell performed in the interim between LBO and merger into VF? Management never said, being private, of course. The higher value of the company to VF—Blue Bell's LBO investors had paid only $10 a share and sold each for $80 to VF—was mainly the result of reducing their debt load, not because of improved sales and profits.

Then, there was Levi Strauss, king of jeans and much diversified into other apparel categories. In 1985, the Haas family reassumed ownership of its company by making a $1.7 billion LBO. The family already owned 41 percent of the stock but professed to want independence from Wall Street and protection from potential raiders and greenmail artists. Headed by Robert Haas, the family scion, Levi proceeded to severely reduce the company by selling or discontinuing such products as fashion and designer apparel, hats and belts, with the object of returning to its basic product, jeans. Earnings continued, however, helped by the closing of forty plants and a cut of twelve thousand employees. But, using the company's own figures, 48 percent of pretax income from 1986 through 1990 will go just for interest payments on debt.

What was really behind the Haas family's LBO? One may accept the professed desire for independence and for the family to return to a more active philanthropical role. But also to be considered is Levi's risky policy in the 1970s and early 1980s to dramatically expand its distribution to the two retail giants, Sears Roebuck and J. C. Penney, annoying its twelve thousand regular accounts, including Macy's, which summarily dropped the line and launched its own private-label jeans. The upshot was a groundswell of unhappiness and disaffection leading to greater use by loyal retail accounts of other jeans lines.

The greatest example of the difficulties of LBOs involved that of Safeway Stores, the nation's largest supermarket chain. Pushed by a threat from the Haft family (Dart Drugs, Crown Books, and an automotive supply chain), Peter A. Magowan, Safeway chairman and chief executive, began at his succession to the top in 1980 to streamline his vast business, which had $18 billion in sales. This thrust led to the departure of half a dozen top executives and to divestiture of stores in West Germany and Canada. Then, in 1986, Magowan and a group of executives launched a leveraged buyout with a total $4.6 billion of debt. That in turn led to the most massive divestiture of stores in the history of American food retailing since the Great Atlantic & Pacific Tea Company, known as A&P, discontinued more than one-third of its entire national business in the 1970s. The strategy was to return Safeway to its core businesses, both to reap better profits and to pay the huge debt.

In Dallas, Safeway in 1987 sold its 160-store division, then divested its 60 stores in Salt Lake City, its 132 stores in the United Kingdom, and 124 in Australia. And it consolidated a number of its divisions in the eastern United States, merging its 62 stores in Richmond, Virginia, with its 145-store division in Washington, D.C. Viewing the unemployment-strewn terrain left by Safeway, the United Food and Commercial Workers International Union estimated that about fifteen thousand jobs would be lost, more than eight thousand in the Dallas area alone. What was Safeway's eventual goal? Industry speculation was that the Oakland, California, company would have to continue its reduction program until it could pay back at least $3 billion of its $4.6 billion debt. This would leave Safeway able to operate effectively with a mere $1.6 billion debt, it was assumed. Through early 1987, Safeway had been able to raise about $2 billion through the sale or closing of its domestic and foreign stores. That left another $1 billion to be derived from yet more divestiture. Obviously, Peter Magowan, who had had ongoing problems with the food union, meant to cut back further.

Publicly, the company said that it could no longer subsidize unprofitable stores with profitable ones. In an April 1987 interview with *Supermarket News*, the food industry trade paper, Robert Bradford, Safeway senior vice-president, said, "We were moving in that direction all along, working on problems in some divisions and we probably would have turned some of those problems around. But we no longer have the luxury of time because we have bills to pay, and we have to be a going, profitable company. That's why we're evaluating all our assets."

He should have added, too, that with its entry into a leveraged buyout, Safeway's management was under a new, non–Wall Street pressure—that of its bank lenders. Banks aren't like small share-holders or Wall Street analysts, who mostly want just good results. Banks want the loans they extend to be repaid, with interest and on time. Banks want dollars.

And how was Macy's faring in the midst of all this flux?

Finkelstein, Handler, and the other team members were well aware of the trauma and pressure in the field of LBOs. They, too, were straining to produce results and reduce their debt. They knew that not every banker thought they could succeed, particularly since they had been compelled to reduce the $70-a-share offering price to $68 a share in December 1985. "The new price is what the financial markets indicate is the acceptable price," said a spokesman for the buying group. And even as late as March 1986, three months before the shareholders were to approve the buyout, three traditional Macy lenders, Chase Manhattan Bank, the Morgan Guaranty Trust Company, and the Bankers Trust Company, declined to participate in the financing, though Bankers Trust eventually joined the banking syndicate.

But through 1987 and 1988, the Macy team had its buyout, and while the pressure from the thirteenth floor was brutal at times, the buying group was making progress—and praying for all the breaks it could get.

CHAPTER ELEVEN

PRIVATE WORLD

Its own world. That's what Macy's had wrought. Gone were the encounters, heated by rhetoric, the confrontations with the corporate gadflies, the little shareholders with their brightly expectant eyes, the lawyer-shareholders who could spout resentment and legal precedent in the same breath, the Wall Street analysts who carped at every blip in sales or profits, the media that could always be counted on to see things their way, not the right way. Gone were those meetings that made the heart pound.

What a blessing it all was, that private world in the midst of an ever-growing public one. But in some ways it was an illusion.

Between October 19, 1987, Black Monday, the worst day on Wall Street since the great fall that had precipitated the Depression, and January 25, when a feisty, hyperenergetic Canadian named Robert Campeau had mounted a hostile takeover against the august Federated Department Stores, Macy's had few uncomfortable brushes with reality. But those two days had to be memorable ones.

The Black Monday disaster, with its consequent drop of 50 percent in the price of most retail stocks, not to mention those of many other industries, demonstrated that the day when Macy might go public and reward the buyout team with untold riches might be a lot farther off than anticipated. The attack on Federated might have been laughed off except that Campeau had staged a similar and successful foray at Allied Stores Corporation only sixteen months earlier. One had to take it seriously, not just the apparently stunned directors of Federated but Macy's management, too. If anything, it proved to them that they had anticipated such an unfriendly swipe at an establishment company, just as they were, and avoided such a possibility by buying the company themselves, no matter what the critics might say.

So on those two days there was first dismay and then shock followed by elation. And what it showed both Macyites and Macy watchers was that going private only meant buying up shares owned by outsiders— not that the insiders could crawl into a hole and close the cover behind them. In an industry like retailing, where everyone fought for pretty much the same consumer, where Wall Street often called the shots by recommending buying or selling a company's shares, where the growth of imports made domestic suppliers frantic and merchants defensive, there simply was no such thing as a privately run retail company.

Finkelstein had tried to make it one by drawing into a hole after the buyout. By cutting his public information and financial documentation to a trickle, he seemed to have satisfied his desire for insulation from Wall Street analysts with their fickle insistence on short-term performance and from the media with its penchant for the negative and sensational.

He implemented the desired privacy in a number of other ways. He stopped Macy from releasing its sales results every month, as most of the other big retailers did. He said monthly sales were meaningless and much too short-term in their significance. He ordered his controller's office to cease contributing Macy's monthly sales percentage changes to *The New York Times*, a practice that had been followed by Macy's and the other big New York stores for decades. Asked why, he told Marvin Traub, the chairman of Bloomingdale's, that he didn't want his buyers worrying about "market share. I want them to concentrate on profits." How a buyer would be deterred from making a better profit by seeing how his competition was faring was a bit difficult to fathom. A more likely reason was that Finkelstein didn't want his competitors to know how he was doing. Or anyone else, though it is not humanly possible to make any normal, red-blooded buyer cease and desist from wanting to know how he was faring against his competition.

Relationships with suppliers were changed to less frequent contacts and more demands. Producers, many of them already annoyed at the inroads Finkelstein's push on imported private labels was making on their sales at Macy's, were called in and told that they must give the company's buyers even better wholesale prices, add every possible discount and promotion and markdown allowance. Macy's also drew the vendors' ire by spreading out payments beyond the normal terms; they were not alone in this delaying tactic, but the practice added salt to the already inflicted wounds. Seventh Avenue manufacturers talked of nothing else for a time, met to map concerted action, but did little to punish Macy. It was still too big a customer to fight, even though it was generally acknowledged that if Macy's had still been a public company, Finkelstein could not have pushed store labels spewed out by the Far East factories in Hong Kong as he could as head of a private company.

Press relations, never very open since Finkelstein took over the New York division in 1974, worsened and turned stiff and uncomfortable. "No comment" was the standard answer to any question, except on those infrequent occasions when Macy's released a statement, almost always of a favorable nature, and didn't mind elaborating on that—up to a point.

The buyout team, particularly its chief, enjoyed the privacy in which it could operate. Still, there were times when Finkelstein felt it neces- sary to go public, that is, tell the world how well Macy was doing in its leveraged buyout. In November 1986, five months after the share- holders had approved the management purchase, a public relations consultant working for Macy called to ask if I would be interested in an interview on Macy's progress. I had requested such an interview only a few months earlier through the same public relations man but been told "Ed wasn't ready." Surprised by the invitation, since Finkelstein had severely objected to my last story in *The New York Times*, on October 15, 1985, I eagerly accepted the offer. A few days later, Finkelstein and Handler agreed to an interview in which some of the following comments were made by Finkelstein:

"You pretty quickly know if an LBO works. Something goes wrong quickly if it doesn't. But we were very pleased at the intensity of the executive organization. There's no question in my mind that the LBO was the reason. We were a well-run organization before, but once we unleashed the entrepreneurial spirit, the people feel that they own the business and indeed they do own part of it. It's a group that had owned 1.5 percent of Macy's, now it owns 20 percent. We had a festivity celebrating the buyout and we all felt very well about the fact that the people who had built Macy now owned the business. Certainly we are heavily in debt, but our ownership for a total investment of $17.5 million will really be worth something five, seven years down the line," Finkelstein said.

"Many LBOs come in with investors who sell off the assets to pay off the debt. Others come in and see a need to replace the management. We saw an opportunity to keep a well-run company and the management together. If not, well, that would be like 1984–85, when we were losing people and spending an enormous amount of time with the people who stayed to keep them going. You can, of course, do what the baseball teams do—pay an enormous salary and hope that the players will produce. But the big money sometimes reduces the motivation. The beauty of our LBO is that the players get their reward from their performance.

"Recently, I ran into Michel Bergerac, who had just sold Revlon and who I think is just counting his money now. I told him how grateful we, Mark and I and the others, were to him, to Catfish Hunter of the Yankees and Bob Suslow of the Batus Retail Division. All of them got such great deals in remuneration that it changed the whole executive remuneration environment. It made all of us—and all the young people—become very money-minded. And that's what we have to make sure to engender as a motivation.

"For the next several years, our business would grow an average 8 percent a year store-for-store, or a total 10 to 11 percent each year and our profits would average our fine 1983–84 levels," Finkelstein said. "The 1985 profit percentage was an unusual performance. We felt confident we could return to the 1983–84 profits, although our growth rate in sales would be more modest but earnings would continue. From 1979 through 1985, our average annual sales grew about 13.5 percent and we believed our earnings projection would continue at 10 percent pretax."

In its projections for the "surviving corporation," the Macy team presented very ambitious figures over the 1987–1996 decade. The 1987 sales of $5.053 billion would grow to $6.225 billion in 1989, to $7.530 billion in 1991, to $8.973 billion in 1993, and to $11.584 billion in 1996. The bottom-line forecast provided for losses of $63 million in 1987, $38 million in 1988, and $9 million in 1989. Starting in 1990, net profits would return, starting that year with $30 million, with $69 million in 1991, $109 million in 1992, $151 million in 1993, $224 million in 1994, $295 million in 1995, and $377 million in 1996.

What about liabilities, assets, and debt? The total liabilities would grow from $950 million in 1987 to $1.189 billion in 1991 and to $2.043 billion in 1996. Total assets were projected to rise from $4.237 billion in 1987 to $4.827 billion in 1991 and to $5.442 billion in 1996. But, according to the forecasts, long-term debt would rise from $2.991 billion in 1987 to $3.155 billion in 1991 and then drop to $1.504 billion in 1996.

"This was not an asset play," Finkelstein continued. "We had always planned to sell our real estate, as Federated, May, and Dayton Hudson did with their shopping centers. But what we intended to do was reduce our debt ahead of schedule, to do better than the banks expect. That changes the debt-equity relationship and that was our goal. And that is what we are doing."

And the fact was that the new Macy's was doing better in the initial months after the buyout. According to Finkelstein's numbers, sales in the immediate quarter after the buyout, the first quarter ended November 1, 1986, sales rose 16.4 percent, and instead of the $28 million loss foreseen in that period, the deficit was only $8.6 million. But, many observers agreed, it was still too early to call the buyout a success. At least five factors would determine the LBO's real achievement: the financial results, of course; the performance of all the players; how the rest of the uninvested Macy community reacted to it; how many in the buyout group remained and those key executives under them; and how the stock market behaved in preparation for the cash-in, when Macy's went public, probably by 1992.

In the meantime, Finkelstein wanted again—several times, in fact—to part the curtains of his private world. His public relations man got busy. Before *The New York Times* article appeared on January 25, 1987, resulting from two interviews the previous November, stories appeared on November 13, 1986, in *Women's Wear Daily*, noting that Macy's had trimmed its loss, and in the issue of January 12, 1987, of *Business Week*, observing that "the largest LBO in retail history is paying off with a loyal, energized staff and increased business."

In between, *Women's Wear Daily* did another piece, publishing on December 29, 1986, a full two-page article on Macy's, featuring thirteen-inch-high photographs of Finkelstein and Handler, and written by reporter Peter Born.

In February 1986, Management Horizons, one of the nation's most respected retailing consultants, rendered a strategic assessment of

R. H. Macy for Citibank and Manufacturers Hanover Trust Company. It was ordered by both banks to assist them in deciding whether to extend loans in the management acquisition of Macy's, which they ultimately did. In all, it was a considerably favorable assessment, based on a study of the consulting firm's on-site research in areas embracing Macy's divisional presence, its own general research into retailing, materials from trade associations, trade press and stock brokerage analyses, and interviews with Finkelstein and Handler. The report found problems in a lag of the inventory-to-sales ratio, which Management Horizons said was being corrected; the implementation of commission selling in various Macy stores, which management conceded needed "more work"; and the issue of whether Macy needed more divisional or departmental consolidation, which management said was probably not necessary.

In what may be the most intriguing portion of the lengthy report, the consultant's interviews dwelled on the matter of the "dependency on Mr. Finkelstein."

The report said:

> The final issue addressed with management was the reaction to trade press comments that Macy's success is highly dependent on Mr. Finkelstein. As expected, the response was to downplay the concern. However, several comments made during this discussion seem insightful.
>
> Certainly the turnaround from years past was due in large part to Mr. Finkelstein's strategic and merchandising leadership.
>
> The development of the four basic foundations of company strategy has been, in large part, also attributable to the managerial efforts of Mr. Finkelstein and Mr. Handler.
>
> However, the senior management groups at corporate and divisional level have been involved in the refinement and implementation of plans for many years and they seem to be solidly lodged in the "Macy's Way." Today there are strong people in place who have developed a commitment to the strategies and philosophies of Mr. Finkelstein, reducing the dependency on Mr. Finkelstein himself.
>
> Certainly, it is apparent that Mr. Finkelstein is responsible for the evolution of the management acquisition effort.
>
> Management perception today is, however, that due to the structure of the management acquisition including a relatively large group of Macy's executives who have been involved directly in the reemergence of Macy's as an important force in conventional department store retailing, the dependence upon Mr. Finkelstein for the future success of Macy's has been tempered.

That, of course, as Management Horizons took pains to observe, is what Macy's management concluded. It is not, however, what the recent history of American retailing would substantiate. In that ego-intensive business, a strong, dynamic chief executive often has a bad habit of picking weak subordinates who turn out to be weak successors. Tough guys, it seems, don't dance, as Norman Mailer has said, but they do like "yes" men.

Sidney Solomon, the great chairman and chief executive of Abraham & Straus, brought that company to the height of the department store business, but his hand-picked successors didn't last very long and soon had A&S on the ropes. George Farkas, the founder of Alexander's Inc., the big New York promotional chain, dedicated his then excellent business to his four sons, whom he had pressured to give up other careers to come into it. But the company floundered and outsiders, including Donald Trump, became important owners. Eugene Ferkauf, the innovative founder of Korvettes, had a sentimental loyalty to his old East Side buddies and hoped they would run his business, but they couldn't and it was taken over by others who ran it into the ground and eventually closed it down.

Whether that will happen at Macy's is hard to predict, but what does appear true is that its dependence upon Finkelstein is indeed great.

Through late 1986 and into the following two years, Macy continued to open its curtains, almost always to disseminate favorable news.

It confirmed published reports in September 1986 that it was changing the name of its Bamberger's division to Macy's, New Jersey. Later, the same was done in Atlanta, where the Davison's division was altered to Macy's Atlanta. The management team had never liked the use of original names in its acquired divisions and the switch was long over-due. The aims were to foster a more centralized operation and also to seek to gain a greater entrenchment of the corporate name in local markets.

In October 1987, the company announced the first full year's results since its leveraged buyout. Sales for the 1987 fiscal year rose 14.5 percent to $5.21 billion from $4.65 billion the prior year. The compari-son excluded twelve Midwest stores sold to the Dillard Department Store chain when the Kansas City, Missouri-based Macy division was merged into Atlanta. Macy's reported it earned $59.6 million on a pretax basis in that year, against a forecast loss of $42.7 million. When I requested a comparison of earnings for the previous year, the reply was, "It's not meaningful, not available because of a complete financial restructuring." Due to "an unusually high income tax provision," the company said it had a book loss of $13.8 million against a forecast loss of $62.5 million at the time of the buyout.

"Fiscal 1987 was a very good year for Macy's and reflected material improvement over the forecasts used in our planning of the buyout," said Finkelstein in a formal statement. "Our sales were even better than anticipated and interest costs were lower due both to the level of indebtedness and the favorable interest rate environment. Our healthy sales increase provides a strong base as we enter fiscal 1988."

Also in October 1987, Macy opened its third store in Connecticut at the Danbury Fair Mall, a large, 229,000-square-foot unit that represented its deepest penetration into rural Connecticut. The move demonstrated that Macy while still grappling with several billions of dollars of debt, was expanding into new stores. The previous month, Macy announced its entry into the specialty shop field. Three separate chains would be opened, and the first would be named Aeropostale, with two shops in New Jersey and the third in California. The first concept would embrace men's and women's active sportswear, using a private label that Macy had had in its regular stores for some time. The second store type, to be known as Charter Club, would sell another private label line of career-type women's sportswear already stocked at Macy. The third would be called Fantasies and sell intimate apparel.

Since all three shop concepts would sell exclusively Macy's store brands or private labels, the project aroused much attention within the domestic garment industry centered on Seventh Avenue in Manhattan. As Macy's product development effort had geared up to encompass almost 25 percent of the chain's total sales, Finkelstein sought some ways in which to use some of the imports produced in the Far East or arranged for out of his Manhattan "factory." In 1986, he had announced that Macy would offer to sell a wholesale line of some of those labeled goods to other American retailers, and according to trade reports, he offered it to other large chains, such as May Department Stores Company, Dayton Hudson, and Nordstrom Inc. But he learned to his disappointment that they really weren't interested. First, they had their own expensive product-development entities that gave them what they needed. And, second, they told him, it would be unwise for them to offer labels or goods also sold by Macy's, since it would give the impression that they depended upon other retailers for their innovation.

Thus the entry into specialty shops, something that Finkelstein, Handler, and their associates had spurned while almost every other large retailer had ventured into it, was a way of absorbing the vast influx of imports. This raised the question of whether Ed Finkelstein had become the victim rather than the master of the import, private-label machine that he had engineered.

In January 1988, Macy said its New York division would open a 167,500-square-foot store devoted strictly to clothing in Boynton Beach, Florida, in August 1989. It would have only two floors, instead of the usual three that Macy's operated, and it would have no electronics, domestics, bedding, rugs, or furniture, and would not have any "Cellar." But while Macy didn't say so, one may be certain that when it opens it will have plenty of private-label imports.

In that same month of January 1988, Finkelstein happily reported that in the first fiscal quarter ended the prior October 31, Macy's had returned to the black after only one year of losses resulting from the leveraged buyout. It was a small net profit, $6.43 million, but it was compared with a loss of almost $9 million in the comparable, year-earlier quarter. He said again that he expected the 1988 fiscal year to be profitable, two years ahead of schedule. Sales in the quarter rose 9.8 percent, according to the statement Macy filed with the SEC, which it was compelled to do because of its publicly owned bonds. "Comp" store sales, those in stores at least a year old, rose 5.9 percent, resulting from an improved merchandise mix that in turn produced better sales per square foot. But long-term debt remained high (although slightly lower than predicted) at $2.87 billion.

The pressure remained. Again in February 1988 the rumors grew that a top-level executive would defect from the buyout. As a prominent executive recruiter put it, "There's new restlessness in the buyout group. We have heard that a division head may pull out of the whole deal. October 19 reduced the expectations and faith in the leveraged buyout. And despite what the company says, their numbers aren't as sexy as before. The multiple on the buyout's investment used to be eighty times. Now, it's about forty and going lower."

There was, in those early months of 1988, yet another reason for the tension that gripped not only those at Macy's but at many other retailers. The nation's retail business was suffering from the worst erosion of women's apparel sales in years, primarily in the sportswear category. A dearth of fashion innovation had begun stunting sales as far back as the spring of 1987, when the new, short skirt influence suddenly appeared. Bared women's knees and thighs failed to excite interest among already blasé shoppers. It was uncomfortable timing and many retailers declined to accept or push the shortened lengths; supplier-to-retailer pipelines grew clogged.

Both national and private brands felt the harsh indifference of consumers. What had first been a disappointing experience in 1987 with the greatly popular shaker sweater—for three previous years the hottest item in sportswear departments—had spread to skirts, blouses, and jackets. Consumer caution infected retailers and the financial results at the end of 1987 and into 1988 showed it. The Limited, the hottest merchant of women's apparel, had two, back-to-back, declined quarters in profits, sending the usually prescient founder, Leslie Wexner, chasing back and forth to Hong Kong and Columbus to cut back and adjust operations. Brooks Fashions, a large retailer, filed for Chapter 11 bankruptcy proceedings. Petrie Stores, the huge chain of retail shops founded by Milton Petrie, reported several unhappy quarters. And Liz Claiborne, certainly the hottest fashion producer in the country, saw its warehouses building inventories and took the unusual seasonal step of offering retailers a 40 percent discount on its Spring One line and 20 percent on its Spring Two collection.

Bloomingdale's, which should have been able to surmount the apparel business decline and did so because of its popular durables, nonetheless fretted about poor sportswear business. Oddly enough, it wasn't the men's side of the aisle that was hurting, partly because turnover of those goods was half that of women's and expectations weren't as high. Women's sportswear for years had swung the entire business and profits of a typical department store. Now, it was carrying them down.

Again Macy's private world was no desert island. Women's apparel, especially sportswear, slumped as it did everywhere else. Trade rumors insisted that the Macy New York division dropped $1 million in sales in January and that the entire twenty-two-store division was funneling rapidly accumulating inventories through the distant Colonie store, near Albany, New York. Macy's had been steadily running "20 percent off" sales, but now, in an effort to dispose of unwieldy inventories without unduly hurting its image, it was using the Colonie store for that purpose because of its remoteness from the main New York market.

Nonetheless, in its hunger for sales volume, Macy's management had been promoting reduced prices, trying to stay abreast of its import binge and to excite consumers with the hot electronics products to build store traffic. The company's promotional binge prompted a competitive merchant to declare, "Macy's is promoting so much that it makes you wonder how smart Finkelstein is. Pushing price alone doesn't build any loyal customers, just bargain-hunters. They get so used to bargain prices that they tend to ignore the regular-priced goods. I've been in this business for a long time and to me Macy's is just hurting itself. Is that what leveraged buyouts do to you?"

And the head of a large buying office asserted, "Finkelstein's image has become tarnished. He's so rough on suppliers and he's so promotional that he's getting the aura of a merchant driven to excesses. No one is saying that he isn't a great retailer, but he may be in over his head."

Those pressures aside, there was a third reason for concern, a slowly rising tide of disfavor over leveraged buyouts, especially since the October 19 stock market debacle. At the end of January 1988, the Congressional Research Service released a study concluding that increased borrowing of large sums of money by heads of publicly owned companies wanting to take their companies private had led to excessive levels of corporate debt. Such leveraged buyouts could not only be depriving shareholders of significant profits, the study reported, but as a harmful result of such transactions companies had sold or closed large parts of their operations to reduce debt, creating layoffs and reductions in research and development.

The report was accompanied by a statement by a legislator who had requested a report from the research service, an arm of the Library of Congress.

"Rapid growth in leveraged buyouts is of concern particularly, when in the process of going private, corporate managers—supposedly the trustees of the shareholders' assets—use those assets to enrich themselves," Representative John D. Dingell, the Michigan Democrat who headed the House Energy and Commerce Committee, said in *The New York Times* on January 31, 1988. *The Times* added, "Mr. Dingell said he feared that the debt incurred to achieve these buyouts posed a danger to the long-term viability of such companies and that the trend might be diverting key funds away from the stock and bond markets."

In other remarks, the congressman, taking note that LBO advocates called the device a "streamlining of corporate America," said, "For every anecdote describing the efficiency of a leveraged buyout restructuring, there appears to be a case in which large-scale layoffs have occurred and research and development budgets reduced under the weight of debt."

But, as *The Times* put it, "The part of the report that apparently displeased Mr. Dingell the most were the findings that often, after taking a company private, managers returned companies to public ownership through new stock offerings that brought the managers huge personal profits. The practice raises the question of whether shareholders, who are not as aware of the underlying value of a company as its managers, are fairly compensated for their holdings in the company during management's initial offerings."

The issue of what LBOs created naturally led to speculation in the retail industry as to what sort of a company Macy's would have been if its managers hadn't bought it but allowed it to remain a public company. And this became entwined with another issue—is it morally right for a manager invested with the protection of shareholder rights to engage in a takeover of that company?

I asked these questions of many people. Retailers as a rule tended to agree with what Finkelstein, Handler, and the others had done both as a moral and a justifiable personal right; but not all did, including several who thought highly of Finkelstein and still do. Some who approved of what he did said, too, in effect, "I wish I had or could have done it, too. I was paid well but not well enough." A few retailers, fewer in number, thought that what he had done was immoral and improper and counterproductive to Macy. Very few, however, wanted to be quoted by name.

Phil Schlein, the former Macy California chairman and now a principal in U.S. Venture Partners, no friend of Finkelstein, observed, "Macy's isn't any better off. It's worse off. If it had stayed public, it probably could have bought Associated Dry Goods, rather than let May Department Stores have it. Macy could now have been a $10 billion corporation, instead of little more than half that. It would have had five or six more divisions. And I don't think the stores are as exciting as they were. Macy's has become more cautious, no longer taking the fashion risks it should."

David L. Yunich, the former Macy corporate vice-chairman, had much more to say on the subject.

"Was it moral? No. All you have to do is examine any LBO and ask who profits from it. Only the group that engineered it. Not the employees, not the public shareholders, not the community. Only the group that decides to make a run. Finkelstein's argument that someone else might have taken it over is bull. That unless he gave an ownership position to a lot of his key people, he would lose them. That's bull also. He's losing more people now. The shareholders were happy before. There were a lot of widows and orphans in there owning Macy's stock. Certainly they got a $20 premium but only one time. A share of stock is for security, too, not just profit. All you had to do was look at the shareholder's profile and you would see lots of shares left to families from a father or mother who said, or meant to say, 'This is a good stock. It will always give you a good income. Macy's always paid a good dividend.'

"It would only have been morally right," Yunich went on, "if it could be proved that all who were involved with the company would have been better off, that the company would be able to grow faster than it did as a public company, that it would be stronger than if it remained a public company. The answer to all of those questions is no. Macy's is not stronger. It has cut a lot of people. It's milked the assets of the company to load itself up with debt. Who's benefited from the deal? The answer is obvious."

But, to keep things in balance, what about the equity investors?

Michael Price, head of Mutual Shares Company, New York, which invested $45 million in equity of the new Macy, said, "I couldn't be happier. The buying group has integrity, a commitment to the employees. You couldn't have a classier act. The LBO was a way to bring equity to investors in a very classic American way. It's a concept I believe in. Since summer of 1986, the progress has been clearly very good. The only question is how really well they will do."

Peter Solomon, vice-chairman of Shearson Lehman Hutton, the big investment banking house in New York, was initially annoyed that Goldman Sachs wouldn't sell him some of the new Macy bonds. He convinced his firm to buy $3.5 million in equity in the other securities and he and his family took an additional amount. "I could have taken more equity. Most people thought the offer was overpriced. But I thought it was a good deal for the shareholders and for Macy's. It wasn't an immoral thing to do. Absent any real takeover threats, I don't think the stock would have hit $68 a share for some time.

"But there wasn't any real threat," Solomon said. "I think what really drove Finkelstein into the buyout was that he was unable to buy a major retail chain, like Associated Dry Goods or Nordstrom's, because they didn't want to sell. Without that, he decided he had to do something to protect himself and the others."

*   *   *

On March 30, 1990, Ed Finkelstein will reach the age of sixty-five, the age at which top executives often retire. Whether he will be able to leave Macy's as wealthy as he hopes as a result of his leveraged buyout depends on stock market conditions by then. The chances are moderately favorable that those conditions will be conducive to ending Macy's private era and going public again. But what seems certain is that his investment in Macy's will be worth more, probably much more, even if the company is still private. He can always hold on to some or most of his investment by making some special arrangement with his colleagues or sell some or most of it to them at a good premium.

But his legacy to Macy will depend more on what he has accomplished there than on the wealth he accumulated when he generated his internal buyout. It will be a bright legacy, indeed. And then he will go, leaving the company to his successors, which raises a considerably uncertain prospect. Has he created adequate succession? The question is an open one, answered only by the inexorable balance sheet of time itself.

What is likely, however, is that in the 1990s Macy's will be a different company, absorbed once again in the public arena by stock values, takeovers, and competition. It may well merge with or be merged into another company. The private hiatus of the late 1980s will become a footnote in the accountants' remarks in some future annual stockholders' report, whether it bears the name of Macy's or some company that owns Macy's.

And so the dramatic buyout by 350 company employees will be forgotten, perhaps as it should be, as an example of a brief, flickering, impulsive act that aroused envy, heat, and controversy in a time of great change. But its contribution to the ever-growing issue of corporate behavior may well have a much longer life: principles have a way of outliving principals.

EPILOGUE

Only eighteen months after the Macy team had bought the company, an opportunity rose which could have inflated Macy into a company three times its size and accelerated the timetable for the golden cash-in. If some observers expected Macy to merge or be merged in the 1990s, the time had come three years early.

For more than a month, the seventeen directors of Federated Department Stores had been under a state of siege. On January 25, 1988, a financial advertisement appeared in *The New York Times* followed in minutes by an official announcement that informed them that the Campeau Corporation, a large, Canadian builder, was making a $47-a-share offer to acquire Federated. At first blush, it had seemed ridiculous. Robert Campeau, the intense chairman and chief executive of Campeau, had a year earlier acquired Allied Stores Corporation, one of the largest American retailers, for about $3.6 billion and he still had almost $2 billion left in debt to pay for that takeover. His daring move appeared to the Federated board to be something in the nature of a bluff. But when some recalled his doggedness in acquiring Allied—against the vigorous opposition of Allied's management and its partners in defense and financial backers—it dawned on them that Campeau was not to be taken lightly.

He promptly proved it to them by raising his bid $14-a-share, unloosing his attorneys to appeal to the courts, and capturing the publicity initiative. He delivered almost daily verbal bombshells to the media, criticizing Federated's intractability in refusing both his initial and second offers. Instructed by their corporate counsel to hold their tongues as the first five weeks dragged by, Federated's directors appeared to be paralyzed by Campeau's dancing-growling act. However, the Federated board had been busy, as previously undisclosed information shows.

By late February, the directors had prepared a massive, $4-billion purchase offer for about 67 percent of Federated's outstanding common stock. The program had been carefully developed with the approval of Federated's investment bankers, Shearson Lehman Brothers, Goldman Sachs, and Hellman & Friedman, and the law firm, Skadden, Arps, Slate, Meagher & Flom. It was a major defensive tactic to raise the debt level, reduce the assets, and prevent Campeau from buying the majority of the stock. Much of the appropriate bank financing had been lined up and a prospectus was being prepared for a stock buyback at about $65 a share.

But Robert Campeau, who meticulously and instinctively seemed to anticipate every Federated move, again raised his tender offer—to $66 a share—effectively undercutting the Federated strategy.

Federated also had a contingency move to offset the hostile offer—a management-led, leveraged buyout on the order of Macy's. Most outsiders, eagerly awaiting some sort of dramatic rejoinder by Federated (supposedly impregnable to any takeover threat) were becoming frustrated and disappointed by the lack of action. They suspected that the Federated board had insufficient faith in Howard Goldfeder, the chairman and chief executive, because of two consecutive years of reduced earnings in 1984 and 1985 to back him on the LBO. According to Federated sources, such was not the case at all.

Several months before Campeau launched his first shell, the 62-year-old Goldfeder had informed the board that he wanted early retirement, probably within the next year. When Campeau made his hostile attack, Goldfeder told the directors, "As you know, I'm hoping to retire within a year, so my job isn't at stake. But if you wish, I will stay on to help in a recap or leveraged buyout."

But the LBO, like the recapitalization, was based on a stock offering price of up to $65 a share and was doomed to still-birth when Campeau lobbed in his $66-a-share offer.

Goldfeder, however, was not a great success at Federated. A Bloomingdale's alumnus and an effective division chief at both Federated and May Department Stores Company, he had returned to Federated to head its Bullock's division and then aroused the respect of Ralph Lazarus, the chairman and CEO. When family tragedies—Lazarus lost two children in a relatively short time—affected him deeply, Lazarus prevailed on the board to accept his retirement and appoint Goldfeder his successor. Something of a rough-and-tumble merchant, Goldfeder's selection as the first non-family chief of the respected department-store company was a surprise and even a bit of a shock. But from his appointment in 1978, things didn't seem to work right for him. Abraham & Straus, traditionally Federated's most profitable division, fell on hard times because of demographic changes in its two principal markets, Brooklyn and Long Island. A few years later, the big Federated stake in Texas, in the form of both Foley's in Houston and Sanger-Harris in Dallas, found itself in the grip of the oil-industry slump. To grapple with his problems, Goldfeder seized on the concept of delegation, assigning various vice-chairmen to oversee the regional divisions and report to him.

But the network lacked cohesiveness, dynamism, vision. While autonomy is usually effective when the subsidiaries or divisions are strong, it is especially weak when business falters.

For those first five weeks, the directors turned from the abortive recapitalization and LBO to courting other retailers. The May Department Stores Company wanted two Federated divisions, the Foley's stores (by then combined with Sanger-Harris) in Texas and the Filene's fashion stores in Boston, and was willing to pay $950 million. Federated, still hoping to win the takeover war, wasn't interested but Campeau was and made such a deal with May contingent on his winning Federated. The proceeds, later raised to $1.1 billion, would be a core ingredient in obtaining his financing.

Meanwhile, at Macy, Finkelstein cast a mildly covetous eye at some of the Federated divisions: Burdine's in Florida could give him the big, Southern stake he needed to plunge deeply and more quickly into that market. After all, he still had only one Florida store in the Miami suburbs. And he would have loved to acquire the Federated Bullock's division in Los Angeles, giving him a foothold in Southern California to go with the Macy San Francisco group in the north. And, he also mused, the I. Magnin fashion chain owned by Federated would give Macy's a fling into the heady level of fashion retailing for the truly affluent. His own people—Handler, Reiner, and Bobby Friedman—

loved the idea, and, as they saw the Federated directors obviously hard put by their problems, the time for action on their part seemed to have arrived.

At first, according to Macy insiders, Finkelstein called Goldfeder to volunteer help on a possible leveraged buyout. "We've lots of experience that we'll be glad to tell you about," Ed said. But it became unnecessary when the Federated LBO never got off the ground. Then the Macy chief called to ask if Federated would restructure by selling a division or two. Goldfeder made some suggestions but said it was still too early to make any commitments. Then, in the final days of February, it became obvious to Macy that Federated's efforts to find a "white knight" were failing. It became urgent to either jump in or stand aside.

Two others in the Macy camp had thought about it, too: Laurence Tisch, the chairman of Loews Corporation and of CBS Inc., and a substantial Macy investor, and A. Alfred Taubman, the chairman of Taubman Holdings, one of the largest shopping-center developers and chairman of Sotheby Park Bernet Galleries, and also a Macy investor. Late in February at one of their periodic reviews of Macy's, both raised the matter of why Macy didn't take a bigger view of the Federated-Campeau battle. Why not go all the way with a bid for all of Federated?

The next few days were feverish for Finkelstein and his two investment bankers, Drexel Burnham Lambert Inc., and Kidder Peabody. (He had to do without the help of his regular bankers, Goldman Sachs, since it represented Federated.) He and Mark Handler informally polled the 350. Not every one was enthused about a $6 billion bid for Federated when Macy still owed about $2 billion to its lenders on its own leveraged buyout, but the consensus, perhaps swayed by the enthusiasm of the Finkelstein-Handler leadership, was to go for it. And so on February 29, Leap Year day of 1988, Federated found its "white knight." Macy offered a two-tier bid: $73.80 a share for 80 percent of Federated's 90 million shares, and an exchange of the remaining 20 percent for about 40 percent of the stock in a new, combined company. The first step would be financed by borrowed funds; the second by converting the stock of the 350 shareholders of Macy into a new stock in a new public company called Macy's/Federated, Inc.

The proposed transaction meant that Macy would increase its debt from $2 billion to about $8 billion, a mountain of leverage and obligation. But, it would give the company an opportunity to triple its sales and, most important, allow the Macy team to go public immediately.

Within 48 hours, Federated's board embraced the Macy offer, formally approved it and recommended it to the shareholders. Bob Campeau was furious. Macy's bid looked as good or better than his latest
$68 a share across-the-board, but the "back-end," the stock offer,
presented an unknowable factor. Macy said it would specify the value
of the stock later. Rather than expressing concern, the Federated
directors hailed the back-end portion as an opportunity to invest in a
company that would have a golden future. Campeau, supported by
Wall Street "arbitrageurs" who bought stock for a quick cash-in, called
the back-end of the Macy offer deceptive and incalculable, but Finkelstein held firm to the concept.

What ensued over the next month was nothing less than a circus of
competing events, a blur of offensives and defenses which kept participants and observers on edge as Federated brandished its "poison pill"
shareholder rights plan that would allow its shareholders to buy new
preferred stock and seriously dilute the purchases of any attacker.
Three times Campeau's law firm, Cravath, Swaine and Moore, sought
to have the poison pill voided, but a Federal judge insisted that it
allowed Federated's directors to hold "an auction and get the best
price" for the shareholders. Campeau called Federated actions
"repressive," and both Federated and Macy publicly raised doubts
about Campeau's financing ability. When Bob Campeau took a double-
page ad in both *The New York Times* and *The Wall Street Journal* to
describe a litany of aspersions against Macy and Federated, the two
targets launched a libel suit against Campeau.

Events followed quickly. On March 8, Macy also filed a lawsuit
against Campeau to postpone the expiration of its tender offer. On
March 14, Macy, stung by Wall Street complaints that its "back-end"
offer was elusive, sweetened the cash front-end by $200 million to
$77.35 a share for 80 percent of Federated's stock. On March 22,
Campeau boosted its offer to $73 a share and the next day Federated
convened its board to discuss the new Campeau bid. But on March 24,
Federated said it had begun talks with Macy on a possible higher bid to
compete with the new Campeau offer. On March 29, Federated
announced that its board had devised a set of firm guidelines for final
offers to bring the prolonged war to a conclusion and allow "everyone
to get back to work again."

Finkelstein had held steadfast during all those weeks, even though
he was treading in uncertain waters. Campeau was an old campaigner
in takeover terrain, having taken his scars both in Canada and in the

U.S. with a bitterly opposed fight the year before when he had won Allied Stores. Each had strong support from crafty law firms and investment bankers, but for Finkelstein, the situation was more complex. Business was very sluggish in general and at Macy no less than anywhere else. He had his debt hanging over his head, and there were indications that some of his team were impatient and might defect while he was diverted.

Various deals were made by both sides during the fight based on whether each would win. Campeau pushed ahead with his plan to sell the Foley stores and the Filene's fashion stores to the May Department Stores if it succeeded in acquiring Federated. And Federated agreed to sell Macy, just in case Campeau won, the Bullock's stores and the I. Magnin fashion stores, both in California. Finkelstein, spurred by his law firm, also exacted a promise from Goldfeder and the directors to repay his costs of $60 million for the takeover if he lost it. But the real strike in side-deals was Campeau's arrangement to sell Allied's Brooks Brothers' clothing chain to Marks and Spencer, the big British retailer, for $720 million. That agreement with one of the world's most respected merchants sent a shock wave through Federated's board. It did more to establish Campeau's credibility than anything else he had done.

But constant media probing, Wall Street questioning and considerable employee uncertainty raised the issue of how many people would be displaced in either a full takeover or in the contingency side deals both had made. Finkelstein, by his own later admission, found himself waking up at night, seeing vague faces of all the people he might have to fire. It began to dawn on him that perhaps he had gotten in too deeply.

But both he and Campeau had learned something: If you have side deals and you want to raise your bid, raise the cost of the side deal enough to pay for your new offer. And they did. As Bruce Wasserstein, of Wasserstein, Perella and Company, one of Campeau's two investment bankers, put it, "If they didn't have those divestiture deals, the eventual price for Federated would have been a lot less."

The climax to the war came on March 31 after Finkelstein learned that the Federated directors were leaning to the latest Campeau bid. It presented an ignominious conclusion to Macy's dramatic entry into the contest for Federated, especially since the directors had all along preferred Finkelstein's offer because they preferred a merchant buyer over an owner like Campeau. What Finkelstein hadn't realized was that some of the Federated directors were cooling toward him. A few days earlier, he had appeared before the Federated board and perhaps too enthusiastically described the changes, the internal mergers and the potential personnel cuts that would be made at Federated if Macy won. "What it did," a Federated source confided later, "was make the white knight suddenly look like a gray, even a black knight. They began to look at Ed a little differently."

At 7:30 that Thursday morning, Finkelstein phoned with a dramatic plea to give Macy one more chance. "Is there no decency left in corporate America?" he asked the Federated directors in a conference call. That, a new Macy offer of $78.92 a share for the front-end and a choice of either five shares of the merged company or $60 a share for the back-end, and a few threats by a Macy lawyer, held up the auction one more day.

All that day, however, Finkelstein was upset. He felt that he had fully extended Macy with the new higher offer. He was still troubled by the amount of people the Macy's/Federated merger would fire and he was beginning to feel that Robert Campeau was stubborn enough not to quit. And he sensed that the bidding had gotten out of hand. How much further could it go, with someone like Campeau—enough to imperil Macy?

That evening, he invited Campeau to meet him at his Manhattan townhouse on East 77th Street along with their respective lawyers. It was the first face-to-face meeting of the two contenders and it began innocuously enough. "It's nice to meet you," Finkelstein said. "I've been wanting that for some time." Replied Campeau, "I've been wanting that, too." For three hours, they discussed the situation and agreed that the bidding had gone out of control. The lawyers quietly retired to another room. They could hear the two men haggling, shuffling, and walking around the other room. Each asked what it would take for the other to go away. As a Campeau lawyer said later, "What Campeau wanted was too much for Finkelstein to give away. But Bob decided he could live with what Ed wanted." The two shook hands on an agreement for Macy to withdraw on the condition that it be allowed to buy Bullock's and I. Magnin.

The next morning, the Federated board approved a sale to Campeau for $73.50 a share for all the stock. Campeau had his company, Macy had its two new California divisions, and the Federated board had gotten the best deal it could for the shareholders—about double what the stock was worth before Campeau had shown up. All litigation was terminated, and Finkelstein insisted, "I feel terrific. We got a great deal. Actually, we really only wanted those divisions as strategic additions."

To some, his words had a hollow ring. He had entered the arena of merger makers and failed to win, even though he had picked up two trophies. He wasn't the type of executive who ever wanted to lose. But in a brief, telephone interview that final afternoon, he told me that he was glad to be spared the organizational problems and employee dismissals that would have come in the wake of a Federated acquisition. "I would wake up at night and worry about it," he said. "To be saved from that decision is quite a relief."

Looking back on the events of the last two years, it was clearly easier for Finkelstein to effect an internal buyout of his own company, even against some opposition, than it was to buy another. In one, he had the advantage of being an insider. In the other, he was an outsider, knocking on the door but not loudly enough. Campeau's thumping and aggressive financing drowned him out.

The Federated takeover war, however, was to have some dramatic effects on people. Within a month after it was concluded, Campeau had laid off more than 3,600 executives and other employees at Federated and Allied. Macy's takeover of Bullock's was much opposed by its management and associates and its top executives quickly departed. To pay for his enlarged debt, Finkelstein merged both the Macy New York and New Jersey divisions, causing a redundancy of more than 100 junior executives who were then compelled to leave. Bobby Friedman was dispatched to head up the Atlanta division since Art Reiner now chaired the combined New York–New Jersey complex; Theresa Motoris, the Atlanta chairman, was transferred back to New York to head the Macy buying office.

Barbara Bass, who had left Macy's some years earlier to go to Bloomingdale's and then was promoted by Federated to be chairman of I. Magnin, resigned and in her place Finkelstein named Rosemary Bravo, one of the brightest merchandisers at Macy's New York. Eventually, 250 executives were laid off by Macy within weeks by the acquisitions and internal consolidations. Greater centralization was obviously due at Macy to cut expenses and repay the greater debt.

And, in an ironic twist of events, Frank Doroff, whom Finkelstein had advised to be more of a "killer," and who had gone to Bullock's and eventually became its president, spurned Finkelstein's job offer when Bullock's came under the Macy wing. By then, Doroff had established an enviable reputation as a sort of "gentle killer" and aroused the zealous interest of Bob Campeau. Doroff had been entertaining an offer to become chairman of the Neiman-Marcus Group of stores by its largest investor, the General Cinema Corporation, but Campeau dangled a very, luscious promise at Doroff and prevailed on him to become chairman of the Federated buying office in New York. If the young merchandiser would take the job, Campeau said, he would several years hence move him to the top spot at Bloomingdale's, succeeding Marvin Traub on his expected retirement. Sometime in the early 1990s, the man Finkelstein had ousted from his group of "young Turks" would become his biggest, New York competitor.

INDEX

ABOUT THE AUTHOR

Isadore Barmash, the dean of retailing journalists, has covered the Macy's story for *The New York Times*. He is the author of ten books, including *Welcome to Our Conglomerate . . . You're Fired!* He lives in New York City.